"This series is a tremendous resource for those wanting to study and teach the Bible with an understanding of how the gospel is woven throughout Scripture. Here are gospel-minded pastors and scholars doing gospel business from all the Scriptures. This is a biblical and theological feast preparing God's people to apply the entire Bible to all of life with heart and mind wholly committed to Christ's priorities."

BRYAN CHAPELL, President Emeritus, Covenant Theological Seminary; Senior Pastor, Grace Presbyterian Church, Peoria, Illinois

"Mark Twain may have smiled when he wrote to a friend, 'I didn't have time to write you a short letter, so I wrote you a long letter.' But the truth of Twain's remark remains serious and universal, because well-reasoned, compact writing requires extra time and extra hard work. And this is what we have in the Crossway Bible study series *Knowing the Bible*. The skilled authors and notable editors provide the contours of each book of the Bible as well as the grand theological themes that bind them together as one Book. Here, in a 12-week format, are carefully wrought studies that will ignite the mind and the heart."

R. KENT HUGHES, Senior Pastor Emeritus, College Church, Wheaton, Illinois

"*Knowing the Bible* brings together a gifted team of Bible teachers to produce a high-quality series of study guides. The coordinated focus of these materials is unique: biblical content, provocative questions, systematic theology, practical application, and the gospel story of God's grace presented all the way through Scripture."

PHILIP G. RYKEN, President, Wheaton College

"These *Knowing the Bible* volumes provide a significant and very welcome variation on the general run of inductive Bible studies. This series provides substantial instruction, as well as teaching through the very questions that are asked. *Knowing the Bible* then goes even further by showing how any given text links with the gospel, the whole Bible, and the formation of theology. I heartily endorse this orientation of individual books to the whole Bible and the gospel, and I applaud the demonstration that sound theology was not something invented later by Christians, but is right there in the pages of Scripture."

GRAEME L. GOLDSWORTHY, former lecturer, Moore Theological College; author, *According to Plan*, *Gospel and Kingdom*, *The Gospel in Revelation*, and *Gospel and Wisdom*

"What a gift to earnest, Bible-loving, Bible-searching believers! The organization and structure of the Bible study format presented through the *Knowing the Bible* series is so well conceived. Students of the Word are led to understand the content of passages through perceptive, guided questions, and they are given rich insights and application all along the way in the brief but illuminating sections that conclude each study. What potential growth in depth and breadth of understanding these studies offer! One can only pray that vast numbers of believers will discover more of God and the beauty of his Word through these rich studies."

BRUCE A. WARE, Professor of Christian Theology, The Southern Baptist Theological Seminary

KNOWING THE BIBLE

J. I. Packer, Theological Editor
Dane C. Ortlund, Series Editor
Lane T. Dennis, Executive Editor

• • • • • •

Genesis	Psalms	Jonah, Micah, and Nahum	Ephesians
Exodus	Proverbs	Haggai, Zechariah, and Malachi	Philippians
Leviticus	Ecclesiastes		Colossians and Philemon
Numbers	Song of Solomon	Matthew	
Deuteronomy	Isaiah	Mark	1–2 Thessalonians
Joshua	Jeremiah	Luke	1–2 Timothy and Titus
Judges	Lamentations, Habakkuk, and Zephaniah	John	
Ruth and Esther		Acts	Hebrews
1–2 Samuel	Ezekiel	Romans	James
1–2 Kings	Daniel	1 Corinthians	1–2 Peter and Jude
1–2 Chronicles	Hosea	2 Corinthians	1–3 John
Ezra and Nehemiah	Joel, Amos, and Obadiah	Galatians	Revelation
Job			

• • • • • •

J. I. PACKER is Board of Governors' Professor of Theology at Regent College (Vancouver, BC). Dr. Packer earned his DPhil at the University of Oxford. He is known and loved worldwide as the author of the best-selling book *Knowing God*, as well as many other titles on theology and the Christian life. He serves as the General Editor of the ESV Bible and as the Theological Editor for the *ESV Study Bible*.

LANE T. DENNIS is President of Crossway, a not-for-profit publishing ministry. Dr. Dennis earned his PhD from Northwestern University. He is Chair of the ESV Bible Translation Oversight Committee and Executive Editor of the *ESV Study Bible*.

DANE C. ORTLUND is Executive Vice President of Bible Publishing and Bible Publisher at Crossway. He is a graduate of Covenant Theological Seminary (MDiv, ThM) and Wheaton College (BA, PhD). Dr. Ortlund has authored several books and scholarly articles in the areas of Bible, theology, and Christian living.

COLOSSIANS AND PHILEMON

A 12-WEEK STUDY

▲

Christopher A. Beetham

 **CROSSWAY**

WHEATON, ILLINOIS

TABLE OF CONTENTS

SERIES PREFACE

KNOWING THE BIBLE, as the series title indicates, was created to help readers know and understand the meaning, the message, and the God of the Bible. Each volume in the series consists of 12 units that progressively take the reader through a clear, concise study of one or more books of the Bible. In this way, any given volume can fruitfully be used in a 12-week format either in group study, such as in a church-based context, or in individual study. Of course, these 12 studies could be completed in fewer or more than 12 weeks, as convenient, depending on the context in which they are used.

Each study unit gives an overview of the text at hand before digging into it with a series of questions for reflection or discussion. The unit then concludes by highlighting the gospel of grace in each passage ("Gospel Glimpses"), identifying whole-Bible themes that occur in the passage ("Whole-Bible Connections"), and pinpointing Christian doctrines that are affirmed in the passage ("Theological Soundings").

The final component to each unit is a section for reflecting on personal and practical implications from the passage at hand. The layout provides space for recording responses to the questions proposed, and we think readers need to do this to get the full benefit of the exercise. The series also includes definitions of key words. These definitions are indicated by a note number in the text and are found at the end of each chapter.

Lastly, to help understand the Bible in this deeper way, we urge readers to use the ESV Bible and the *ESV Study Bible*, which are available in various print and digital formats, including online editions at esv.org. The *Knowing the Bible* series is also available online.

May the Lord greatly bless your study as you seek to know him through knowing his Word.

J. I. Packer

Lane T. Dennis

WEEK 1: OVERVIEW

▲

▶ **Getting Acquainted**

Paul's letter to the Colossians is a jewel of Christian Scripture. Only four chapters long, it is easy to read through in one sitting, yet it provides stunning vistas of the perfections of Christ that few other New Testament documents can match in such short space. Its majestic hymn of Christ at 1:15–20 is rivaled only by that of Philippians 2:5–11. The letter therefore provides a feast for the theologian to digest. Yet Colossians also pulsates with a message that, despite the limits of the situation for which it was originally written, remains as relevant and significant as ever.

Written at the same time, Philemon is a short companion letter to Colossians. Often neglected, Philemon's impact is out of all proportion to its size. Twenty-five verses long, Philemon was one of the key biblical texts that guided the church in its struggle for the abolition of slavery in the eighteenth and nineteenth centuries in the West. Paul's rhetorical skill, as well as his heart, are clearly on display here as he seeks reconciliation between Philemon and his runaway slave Onesimus. (For further background, see the ESV *Study Bible*, pages 2289–2292; 2353–2354; available online at esv.org.)

▶ **Placing Colossians and Philemon in the Larger Story**

In the beginning, the Creator-King appointed humanity to be his image-bearers, to establish the earth as the realm of the kingdom of God. Heaven and earth would intersect, and God would dwell among a flourishing human community. The will of God would be done on earth as it was in heaven. But humanity rebelled against their King and plunged the world into sin and death. Yet God's original intention for humanity was not to be thwarted. He called Abraham and promised that from this family all the nations of the earth would be blessed (Gen. 12:3). From Abraham descended the nation Israel, which was to carry this blessing to the nations. But the Old Testament story is largely of Israel's failure to accomplish this vocation. In the fullness of time, however, God sent Jesus, Israel's ultimate king ("Messiah"), who, having dealt with humanity's sin forever at his cross and resurrection, took up Israel's stalled mission. In him, the redeemed people of God—comprised now of Jew and Gentile—take up this vocation of Old Testament Israel, bringing the good news of God's reign in Christ to the nations. (Paul's letters to the Colossians and to Philemon fit here.) At the end of history, Jesus will return as the world's King to consummate God's original intention for creation and to establish the kingdom of God fully upon the earth in the new creation. Then God will finally and fully dwell among his people forever.

Key Verse

"If then you have been raised with Christ, seek the things that are above, where Christ is, seated at the right hand of God" (Col. 3:1).

Date and Historical Background

Paul probably wrote his letters to the Colossians and to Philemon while imprisoned in Rome, about AD 61 (although an imprisonment in Ephesus in the mid-50s must remain a possibility). The apostle had already completed the three missionary journeys recorded in the book of Acts (ca. AD 46–57; see 13:1–21:16). After Paul's arrest in Jerusalem and two years of imprisonment in Caesarea, a centurion guard escorted Paul by ship to Rome (Acts 21:27–27:1). After a hazardous journey, he arrived there in the spring of AD 60 (Acts 27:2–28:16). Here he lived under house arrest, although he was able to receive guests (Acts 28:17–31). This first Roman imprisonment lasted at least two years (AD 60–62; Acts 28:30). During this time, he wrote not only Colossians and Philemon but also the letters to the Ephesians and the Philippians. Timothy possibly served as his amanuensis (writing secretary) while Paul dictated the letters (Col. 1:1; 4:18; Philem. 1). Tychicus carried the letters from Rome to Colossae as the apostle's delegate (Col. 4:7–8).

> **Outline**

Colossians

    I. Paul's Greeting of and Thanksgiving for the Colossians (1:1–8)
        A. Paul Greets the Colossian Church (1:1–2)
        B. Paul Thanks God for the Colossians' Faith and Love (1:3–8)
    II. Paul's Prayer for the Colossians (1:9–14)
        A. Paul Prays That God May Fill the Colossians with Knowledge of His Will (1:9)
        B. The Goal of Paul's Prayer: Lives Fully Pleasing to God (1:10a)
        C. Attainment of the Goal: The Four Ways to a Life Fully Pleasing to God (1:10b–12a)
        D. Reasons to Live a Life Fully Pleasing to God (1:12b–14)
    III. The Christ-Hymn and Its Application to the Colossians (1:15–23)
        A. The Christ-Hymn: The Son's Preeminence over all Creation (1:15–17)
        B. The Christ-Hymn: The Son's Preeminence over the New Creation (1:18–20)
        C. The Christ-Hymn Applied: God Has Reconciled the Colossians to Christ (1:21–23)
    IV. Paul's Apostolic Ministry and Its Application to the Colossians (1:24–2:5)
        A. Paul's Apostolic Suffering and Stewardship on Behalf of the Church (1:24–25)
        B. The Mystery of Christ (1:26–27)
        C. The Way Paul Fulfills His Apostolic Charge, and Its Goal (1:28–29)
        D. Paul's Apostolic Labor on Behalf of the Colossian Church (2:1–3)
        E. The Goal of Paul's Instruction: "Let No One Deceive You" (2:4–5)
    V. Paul Confronts the False Teaching (2:6–23)
        A. "Walk in Him": Paul's Programmatic Statement (2:6–7)
        B. "See to It That No One Takes You Captive": The Warning against the Heresy (2:8)
        C. Fullness of Salvation in Christ: Four Reasons to Resist the Empty Heresy (2:9–15)
        D. "Let No One Condemn You": Old Covenant Regulations and Visionary Experience (2:16–19)
        E. Dead with Christ to Demonic Powers, the Fallen Age, and Man-Made Religion (2:20–23)
    VI. Exhortation: Seek Instead the Things of Christ Above (3:1–17)
        A. Reshaping Reality: The Resurrected and Reigning Christ (3:1–4)
        B. Strip Off the Fallen Old Humanity, with Its Vices (3:5–11)
        C. Put On the New Humanity, with Its Virtues (3:12–17)
    VII. Instructions for Relationships both inside and outside the Faith (3:18–4:6)
        A. Wives and Husbands (3:18–19)
        B. Children and Parents (3:20–21)
        C. Slaves and Masters (3:22–4:1)
        D. Exhortation to Missional Prayer (4:2–4)
        E. Walk Wisely to Attract Outsiders (4:5–6)
    VIII. The Letter's Conclusion: Greetings and Final Instructions (4:7–18)

Philemon

    I. Paul's Greeting of and Thanksgiving for Philemon (vv. 1–7)
        A. Paul Greets Philemon (vv. 1–3)
        B. Paul Thanks God for Philemon's Love and Faith (vv. 4–7)
    II. Paul's Appeal concerning Onesimus (vv. 8–25)
        A. Paul Begins His Appeal concerning Onesimus (vv. 8–12)
        B. Reason for the Appeal: Paul's Desire to Have Onesimus as a Personal Aide (vv. 13–14)
        C. Introducing the New Onesimus: "Beloved Brother" Forever (vv. 15–16)
        D. The Appeal Proper (vv. 17–20)
        E. Encouragement to Follow Through on the Appeal (vv. 21–22)
        F. The Letter's Conclusion: Greetings and Blessing (vv. 23–25)

As You Get Started

What is your present understanding of how Colossians and Philemon help us to grasp the whole storyline of the Bible?

What is your current understanding of how Colossians and Philemon contribute to Christian theology? How do these letters clarify our understanding of God, Christ, sin, and salvation?

What aspects of the message of Colossians or Philemon remain unclear for you? Are there any specific questions that you hope to have answered through this study?

As You Finish This Unit . . .

Take a moment to ask God to bless you with increased understanding and a transformed heart as you begin this study of Colossians and Philemon.

WEEK 2: PAUL'S GREETING OF AND THANKSGIVING FOR THE COLOSSIANS

Colossians 1:1–8

The Place of the Passage

Writing a letter that follows typical Roman convention, Paul begins his correspondence to the Colossian church with a formal greeting (Col. 1:1–2) and a thanksgiving for them (vv. 3–8). He has, however, infused both of these epistolary elements with robust Christian content. Paul writes as an "apostle of Christ Jesus," thereby establishing his authority as the Colossians' apostle, despite having neither planted their church nor met them personally (2:1). For the faithful disciples at Colossae, such a letter from the "apostle of the Gentiles" would have been a source of joy, as they sought to remain true to God despite the encroaching "philosophy" with which they had been confronted (2:8). Paul's thanksgiving to God for their faith in Christ and love for fellow disciples would have honored them. Paul also noted that Epaphras, who first brought the message to them, had handed on to them the true gospel. They could be reassured that they had embraced the genuine apostolic tradition (1:7–8).

> ## The Big Picture

In Colossians 1:1–8, the apostle Paul greets the Colossian church and thanks God for them, because of the fruit that the gospel is producing in them since the day it arrived through the ministry of Epaphras.

> ## Reflection and Discussion

Read through the passage. Then review the questions below and write your notes on them concerning this introductory unit of Colossians. (For further background, see the *ESV Study Bible*, page 2293; available online at esv.org.)

1. Paul Greets the Colossian Church (1:1–2)

In view of the dangerous false teaching that has occasioned the writing of the letter, why do you think Paul introduced himself as an "apostle of Christ Jesus" to the gathered Colossian disciples? What is an "apostle"?[1]

As in five other letters of Paul, Timothy is named as Paul's coauthor (see 2 Cor 1:1; Phil. 1:1; 1 Thess. 1:1; 2 Thess. 1:1; Philem. 1). He is mentioned nowhere else in Colossians, yet we know from elsewhere that Timothy served as a delegate of the great apostle (Acts 16:1–3; 17:14–15; 19:22; 20:4; Rom. 16:21; 1 Cor. 4:17; 2 Cor. 1:19; Phil. 2:19; 1 Thess. 3:2, 6; see also 1–2 Timothy). In light of the last sentence of Colossians (4:18), what role may Timothy have played in the composition of the letter? In view of Paul's unapologetic reliance on faithful coworkers to advance the gospel, what might the implications be for Christian life and ministry today?

In his greeting, Paul wishes the Colossians "grace ... and peace from God" (1:2b). Paul has substituted a Christian epistolary blessing for the conventional Roman one ("greetings!"). "Grace" in Paul is a significant concept, here signifying God's kind, saving disposition toward those in Christ. The Greek term for "peace" almost always translates the Old Testament's *shalom*, which conveys more than the absence of conflict. Rather, it signifies wholeness, order, and sound relationship. God established peace through the cross of Christ (1:20). Once at enmity with God, Christians now enjoy this undeserved peace (1:21–22; see Rom. 5:1). Yet Paul desires his audience to experience more of God's grace and peace. How might the very act of reading (or hearing) Paul's letter convey the grace and peace that Paul desired for them in view of the dangerous false teaching?

2. Paul Thanks God for the Colossians' Faith and Love (1:3–8)

Paul overflows with thankfulness to God for the Colossians' faith in Christ and their love for the community of faith. Yet, why does Paul thank *God* for the presence of such faith and love among the community, when it is the *Colossians* who are following Christ faithfully and laboring in love on behalf of others? How might the mention of "love" again at the end of the paragraph, enabled "in the Spirit," help guide you to an answer (v. 8)?

Reread verses 4–5a, looking for the three virtues so central to Paul's thought (see Rom. 5:1–5; 1 Cor. 13:13; 1 Thess. 1:3; 5:8). What are the three? Note Paul's logic concerning "love" and "hope." How does the Colossians' "hope" of partaking in the everlasting kingdom of God *in the future* fuel their ability to labor in love for others *in the present?*

In Colossians 1:6, Paul informs the Colossians that the gospel was advancing across the world. (Its epicenter was Jerusalem; see Acts 1:8.) When it reached Colossae it swept up his audience in its triumphal wake, as it rang out in expanding circles across the Roman empire. Approximately 30 years after the death and resurrection of Christ, the gospel had created numerous communities, whose members swore allegiance to Jesus as Lord. Evidence exists of churches scattered across Palestine, Cyprus, Syria, Asia Minor, Macedonia, Achaia, and Italy by this time. Nearly 2,000 years later, approximately 2.2 billion people across the globe self-identify as Christian or are at least affiliated with a Christian church. That is roughly 32 percent of the global population! Take a minute to ponder this remarkable growth of the gospel. Reflect, too, upon the time you yourself first "understood the grace of God in truth" (Col. 1:6) and thus were swept up in its triumphal advance across the earth.

In verses 7–8, we learn that Paul did not plant the church at Colossae. A Colossian named Epaphras brought the gospel to them. (He possibly also brought it to the nearby cities of Laodicea and Hierapolis; see 4:12–13 and the map on p. 2292 of the *ESV Study Bible.*) Epaphras has traveled to Rome, apparently to ask for counsel regarding the false teaching, and found Paul in his prison. He has therefore journeyed at least a thousand miles for Paul's help. What do you think motivated Epaphras to hazard such a trip? Consider your own estimation of Christ, the gospel, and the people of God. How precious are they to you? In what possible ways in your current circumstances might "love in the Spirit" be leading you to acts of sacrificial devotion to ensure that others have or retain the true gospel?

Read through the following three sections on *Gospel Glimpses*, *Whole-Bible Connections*, and *Theological Soundings*. Then take time to consider the *Personal Implications* these sections may have for you.

▶ Gospel Glimpses

THE GOSPEL OF THE GRACE OF GOD. Paul wrote to the Colossians that the message they had received concerned "the grace of God" (1:6). At its core, the gospel is a message of grace. The phrase is shorthand for the loving, undeserved (and unstoppable) initiative of God launched in Christ to save a world enslaved to sin, demonic powers, and false worldview systems and structures.

THE GOSPEL OF TRUTH. The Colossians heard "the word of truth, the gospel" (1:5). Despite postmodern assertions to the contrary, the message of Colossians asserts that there is absolute truth. The gospel claims to tell the true story of the whole world. Not all truth claims are equally valid. Paul was deeply concerned about a false worldview that threatened to cut the Colossians off from Christ. Love walks hand-in-hand with truth (1 Cor. 13:6; Eph. 4:15). We love neither God nor our neighbor when we bow the knee to the god of relativism.

THE FRUIT-BEARING GOSPEL OF FAITH, HOPE, AND LOVE. Paul writes, "in the whole world [the gospel] is bearing fruit and increasing" (Col. 1:6). This phrase certainly included growth in the number of people coming to faith in Christ across the Roman empire. Yet it also stresses the gospel's dynamic nature, as it generates virtues and holy affections in the people who embrace it. The gospel, by the enabling power of the Spirit, creates communities marked by the fruit of faith, hope, and love (compare Gal. 5:22–23). The gospel is not merely a message about forgiveness; it re-creates people to be all that God originally intended them to be.

Whole-Bible Connections

JESUS, MESSIAH. In Colossians 1:1, Paul calls the Lord "Christ Jesus," while in verse 3 he calls him, "Jesus Christ." Paul's ability to switch the word order of the Lord's appellation is a key indication that the term "Christ" is not in fact Jesus' name at all but rather a title (like "King George"). "Christ" is the English translation of the Greek word *christos*, "anointed (one)," which in turn translates the Hebrew *mashiach* ("messiah"). Recognition that the word "Christ" is a title, and not a surname, reminds us that Jesus is the long-awaited royal Messiah, the ultimate Davidic king. The ascription of the title to Jesus ties him into an Old Testament theme that had been developing for centuries. Numerous Old Testament texts yearn for and promise an ultimate king from the lineage of David, who would establish God's heavenly dominion upon the earth (e.g., Ps. 2; 72; 110; 132; Isa. 9:6–9; 11:1–10; Amos 9:11–12). The fountainhead of this tradition is found in the divine promise to David in 2 Samuel 7:12–16 that his lineage would rule over Israel forever.

KINSHIP BY COVENANT. In the Old Testament, God became "Father" to Israel in the ratification of the Abrahamic and Mosaic covenants (see e.g., Ex. 4:22–23; Deut. 32:5–6; Isa. 63:16; Hos. 11:1). In the ancient Near East, the establishment of a covenant created a familial relationship between two parties who were otherwise biologically unrelated. In the New Testament, Christians are members of the new covenant (Luke 22:20; 1 Cor. 11:25; 2 Cor. 3:4–6; Heb. 8:6–13). By virtue of our participation in this covenant, God has become "our Father" (Col. 1:2). As our Father, he promises to provide for and protect us, as well as to bless us with his presence, until we are safely home in the kingdom of God.

"BE FRUITFUL AND MULTIPLY." The language of the gospel "bearing fruit and increasing" in the whole world (1:6) echoes an Old Testament development that begins at Genesis 1:28. God's original intention for humanity was that they would "be fruitful and multiply" and fill the earth with the rule of God as his image (Gen. 1:26–28). When Adam and Eve rebelled against God, sin and death entered and ravaged God's world. Through the gospel, however, God is re-creating a people to be his faithful image-bearers (Col. 3:9–10).

Theological Soundings

THE TRINITY. In Colossians 1:1–8, all three persons of the Trinity are mentioned. God is mentioned as the Father (vv. 2, 3). Jesus Christ, the Son of God, is mentioned several times. His preexistence and divinity will be stressed later in the letter (1:15–19; 2:9). The Holy Spirit is mentioned at 1:8. From its inception, the Christian movement has claimed that there is only one God, who yet had entered the world in the persons of the Son and the Spirit. It is the raw data of such texts as Colossians 1:1–8 that compelled later theologians to develop more fully the doctrine of a triune God.

THANKSGIVING. In focusing on the details of the text at verses 3–8, it would be easy to lose sight of the forest for the trees. The text is Paul's thanksgiving to God for all he has done by the gospel in Colossae. Thanksgiving and exhortations to thanksgiving run throughout the letter (1:3–8, 12; 2:7; 3:15, 17; 4:2). Thankfulness is commanded because it reminds us of our utter dependence on God. He is the all-sufficient author and giver of life. We, on the other hand, are dependent on him for everything. Thanksgiving glorifies God because it puts the spotlight on the one who deserves the praise for needs met and blessings conferred. It is a fundamental aspect of what it means to be Christian.

▶ Personal Implications

Take time to reflect on the implications of Colossians 1:1–8 for your life. Consider what you have learned that might lead you to praise God, repent of sin, and trust in his gracious promises. Make notes below on the personal implications for your walk with the Lord of the (1) *Gospel Glimpses*, (2) *Whole-Bible Connections*, (3) *Theological Soundings*, and (4) this passage as a whole.

1. Gospel Glimpses

2. Whole-Bible Connections

3. Theological Soundings

---

4. Colossians 1:1–8

As You Finish This Unit . . .

Take a moment to ask for the Lord's blessing as you continue this study. Take a moment also to review this unit, to reflect on some key things that the Lord may be teaching you—and perhaps to highlight for review in the future.

Definition

[1] **Apostle** – Means "one who is sent" and refers to one who is an official representative of another. In the NT, the word refers specifically to those whom Jesus chose to represent him.

WEEK 3: PAUL'S PRAYER FOR THE COLOSSIANS

Colossians 1:9–14

The Place of the Passage

Because he has heard from Epaphras of their faith in Christ and their love for one another (Col. 1:3–8), Paul reports how he and Timothy have begun to intercede for the Colossian faithful. He prays that they might "walk in a manner worthy of the Lord, fully pleasing to him" (v. 10). The means to attaining this goal is their grasp of the knowledge of God's will, consisting in wisdom from the Spirit (v. 9). Basic to this knowledge of God is a firm understanding of the person of Christ in his preeminence[1] over all things. Paul will provide this necessary knowledge about Christ in the next section with the "Christ-Hymn" (1:15–20).

The Big Picture

In Colossians 1:9–14, Paul reports the content of the prayer that he and Timothy offer on behalf of the Colossians so that they might become fully pleasing to the Lord in every way.

▶ **Reflection and Discussion**

Read through the text for this study. Then interact with the following questions and record your notes on them concerning this section of Paul's letter. (For further background, see the *ESV Study Bible*, pages 2293–2294; available online at esv.org.)

1. Paul Prays That God May Fill the Colossians with Knowledge of His Will (1:9)

When Epaphras brought them news of the success of the gospel at Colossae, Paul and Timothy began a regular ministry of intercession for this new Christian community. How about your prayer life? Do you take time to intercede regularly for other followers of Christ? What obstacles possibly stand in your way from embracing such a ministry? How might Paul's prayer provide a pattern for your own prayers?

Paul prays that the Colossians might grasp the will of God concerning how they are to conduct their lives. Paul writes that such knowledge consists in "all spiritual wisdom and understanding." What do you think "spiritual" might mean in this context? Where does this wisdom come from (compare Ex. 31:3; 35:31; Deut. 34:9; Isa. 11:2; and see the *ESV Study Bible* notes on these passages).

------

2. The Goal of Paul's Prayer: Lives Fully Pleasing to God (1:10a)

Paul intercedes with a specific purpose in view. He prays for the Colossians that they might "walk in a manner worthy of the Lord, fully pleasing to him." Note that "the will of God" is not tied to specific guidance for the uncertain future (e.g., "Lord, whom should I marry?" or "Where shall I go to college?"). Rather it consists in knowable, concrete, righteous, ethical conduct. Are there any areas of your "walk" with God that are inconsistent with what you know to be God's will? If so, what do you intend to do about the incompatibility of what you know to be God's will and the way you are living?

3. Attainment of the Goal: The Four Ways to a Life Fully Pleasing to God (1:10b–12a)

In verses 10b–12a, Paul explains more precisely what is involved in living a life that is fully pleasing to God. The first way is to live a life that is "bearing fruit in every good work" (v. 10b). The New Testament is clear that, while we are not saved *by* our good works, we are saved *for* good works (see, e.g., Eph. 2:8–10; Titus 2:14; 3:5). Reflect upon your own life. Over the course of your life as a Christian have you seen growth, as in the life of a fruit tree, in bearing the good works and fruit of the Spirit (Gal. 5:22–23)?

Paul writes that the second way of living a life worthy of God is to live "increasing in the knowledge of God" (Col. 1:10c). The phrase "knowledge of God" derives from the Old Testament (Hos. 4:1; 6:6). It does not merely pertain to head knowledge about God but also resonates with overtones of covenant relationship and the loyalty that God expects from his people. Reflect on your own life. Are you growing in "knowledge of God" in this sense (i.e., commitment to God)?

In Colossians 1:11, Paul spells out the third aspect of living a life fully pleasing to God. Having been "strengthened with all power, according to his glorious might," Christians are to live a life of "endurance" and "patience." "Endurance" pertains to the ability to remain faithful to God even amid difficult circumstances. "Patience" is the capacity to tolerate delays or problems, including dealings with people who may be irritating or difficult. Reflect for a moment on where the strength comes from for such endurance and patience. What does the text say?

In verse 12a, Paul explains the final element of a life that is fully pleasing to God. Christians are to be characterized by thankfulness (see also 1:3; 2:7; 3:15, 17; 4:2). Gratitude before God is forever fitting because of all that God has done for his people in Christ (vv. 12b–14). Gratitude protects a heart from complaining and grumbling, which are symptoms of dissatisfaction with God (see e.g., Phil. 2:14). Where are you in the life of thankfulness? What steps might you take to grow in gratitude?

4. Reasons to Live a Life Fully Pleasing to God (1:12b–14)

In Colossians 1:12b–14, Paul lists reasons why the Colossians should be marked by lives of thankfulness "to the Father." Read this text again. List the reasons Paul gives for why their lives ought to be marked by ceaseless gratitude. Consider how the reasons also apply to you and provide you with grounds for thankfulness.

Read through the following three sections on *Gospel Glimpses, Whole-Bible Connections*, and *Theological Soundings*. Then take time to consider the *Personal Implications* these sections may have for you.

Gospel Glimpses

DELIVERANCE. At the center of the gospel is a God who reached down to rescue humanity enslaved to the satanic dominion of darkness that had overrun the world. At the cross of Christ, the Father delivered us from this domain and transferred us into the kingdom of his Son, the Lord Jesus Christ (Col. 1:13).

THE FORGIVENESS OF SINS. Elsewhere in Colossians, Paul explains that we "once were alienated and hostile in mind, doing evil deeds" (1:21). As estranged and hostile enemies of God, our treason against the Creator-King deserved eternal condemnation. But God has reconciled us to himself through Jesus Christ, making peace with us by his death on the cross (1:20, 22). For all those who embrace the gospel's message, God offers "the forgiveness of sins"—past, present, and future (1:14).

Whole-Bible Connections

THE ULTIMATE EXODUS. Several words and phrases in 1:12–14 echo language of the Old Testament and God's deliverance of the Hebrews from Pharaoh and Egypt (see Exodus 1–15). The language of "redemption" and "deliverance" from the "domain of darkness," being "transferred" into "the kingdom of his beloved Son," and having a "share" of the "inheritance" of the people of God all recall this act. The exodus stands as the foundational deliverance in the Old Testament. In Christ, however, God has delivered his people in an ultimate exodus redemption, not rescuing them merely physically from an earthly superpower but from the satanic empire of spiritual darkness and death.

THE DAVIDIC MESSIAH-KING. The phrase "the kingdom of his beloved Son" (Col. 1:13) echoes language from the Old Testament. In 2 Samuel 7:12–16, God promised King David that the lineage of his sons would rule over the kingdom of Israel forever. God installed David's son, Solomon, as the initial fulfillment of this promise. The Lord had set his love upon Solomon, whose alternate name thus became Jedidiah, meaning "beloved of God" (2 Sam. 12:24–25). According to Colossians 1:13, Jesus Christ is David's ultimate son. As the "beloved," God has chosen him to reign over the kingdom of God upon the earth forever in ultimate fulfillment of the promise to David.

Theological Soundings

PRAYER AND GROWTH. Paul prayed regularly for the Colossian Christians, asking God for their spiritual growth. Paul clearly presupposed that God would hear these prayers and bring about growth, since this was in accord with God's will (1:9–10; see John 15:7–8). In the mysterious wisdom of his providence, God has ordained that intercessory prayer be a means of growth in grace for disciples of Christ. We dare not neglect such a powerful tool as we seek the spiritual health and growth of the global church.

THE TRINITY AND SALVATION. As in the previous unit, we once again detect here the presence of each of the three persons of the Trinity. In Colossians 1:9–14, we catch a glimpse of their respective work in regard to the plan of salvation. The Father delivers us from the domain of darkness and transfers us into the kingdom of his Son (v. 13). The Son is the person in whom we have "redemption, the forgiveness of sins" (v. 14). The Spirit, only faintly detected in the passage, is nevertheless present as the source of all true "wisdom and understanding" and growth in the knowledge of the will of God (see v. 9, where "spiritual" means "of the Spirit").

Personal Implications

Take time to reflect on the implications of Colossians 1:9–14 for your life. Consider what you have learned that might lead you to praise God, repent of sin, and trust in his gracious promises. Make notes below on the personal implications for your walk with the Lord of the (1) *Gospel Glimpses*, (2) *Whole-Bible Connections*, (3) *Theological Soundings*, and (4) this passage as a whole.

1. Gospel Glimpses

2. Whole-Bible Connections

3. Theological Soundings

4. Colossians 1:9–14

As You Finish This Unit . . .

Take a moment to ask for the Lord's blessing as you continue this study. Take a moment also to review this unit, to reflect on key things that the Lord may be teaching you—and perhaps to highlight these for review in the future.

Definition

[1] **Preeminence** – The quality of being first, foremost, or of highest significance. In the Bible, this quality is attributed supremely to Christ (Col. 1:18).

WEEK 4: THE CHRIST-HYMN AND ITS APPLICATION TO THE COLOSSIANS

Colossians 1:15–23

▲

The Place of the Passage

Having thanked God for the success of the gospel among the Colossians, as evidenced by the existence of Spirit-produced faith, hope, and love (Col. 1:1–8), and having reported the contents of his prayer for them (1:9–14), Paul now introduces a hymn about Christ and applies its message of cosmic reconciliation to the Colossians (1:15–23).

The Big Picture

In Colossians 1:15–23, Paul introduces a hymn that extols Christ's preeminence over both creation and the inaugurated new creation by virtue of his unique role in God's project of cosmic reconciliation. Paul does so to explain to the Colossians that they have been truly swept up into this project, inasmuch as they now display the telltale signs of reconciliation and persevering faith.

▶ Reflection and Discussion

Read through the passage for this study. Then review the questions below and write your notes concerning them. (For further background, see the *ESV Study Bible*, pages 2294–2295; available online at esv.org.)

1. The Christ-Hymn: The Son's Preeminence over All Creation (1:15–17)

While the ESV text does not explicitly demarcate Colossians 1:15–20 as a unique composition within the letter, scholars are virtually certain that the text is a hymn or piece of poetry. Paul has either inserted an existing hymn into his letter or has composed it himself at the time of writing. The hymn divides into two major sections, extolling first the Son's preeminence over creation (vv. 15–17) and then his preeminence over the inaugurated new creation (vv. 18–20). In view of the false teaching at Colossae that Paul understood to dangerously downplay Christ, why do you think Paul introduces this hymn here in the letter?

The phrase that the Son is "the image of the invisible God" may suggest to some a direct allusion to Genesis 1:26–27, and that Paul is teaching that Christ is the ultimate Adam (see Rom. 5:12–21). This is unlikely to be the primary background of the language, however, because the reason given in verse 16 for why the Son is the image is that "by him all things were created . . . all things were created through him and for him." Instead, the probable background is Proverbs 8:22–31 and its development in later Jewish literature. There, the personified figure of wisdom is pictured as having served as God's agent in the act of creation. Paul is explaining that Christ fulfills all that this literary personification signified (compare John 1:1–3; 1 Cor. 8:6; Heb. 1:1–3). The phrase "image of the invisible God" expresses the same idea as Hebrews 1:3, that the Son "is the radiance of the glory of God and the exact imprint of his nature"

28

(compare John 14:9). Try to put in your own words what you think Paul means by saying that the Son is the "image of the invisible God."

In Colossians 1:15, the phrase "the firstborn of all creation" does not mean that there was a time when Christ did not exist; rather, it denotes both his primacy of rank as well as his temporal preeminence over everything in the created order (i.e., his preexistence; see also v. 17a). In view of the erroneous teaching that wrongly exalted heavenly angelic beings, resulting in a denigration of Christ, how does this title ("the firstborn of all creation") function to reassert Christ's supremacy over any being considered as a legitimate contender for his authority (v. 16b; compare 2:8, 10, 15, 18, 20)?

In verse 16, Paul writes that not only is the Son the agent *through* whom God created all things, but he is also the *goal* or purpose for which they all exist ("all things were created through him and *for* him"). Elsewhere in the New Testament, such language is reserved for God alone (Rom. 11:36; 1 Cor. 8:6; Heb. 2:10). Reflect upon what this means—first, for your understanding of Christ, and second, for your own life.

In Colossians 1:17, Paul teaches not only that the Son worked with God to create all things in the beginning, but also that he "continually sustains his creation, preventing it from falling into chaos or disintegrating (cf. Heb. 1:3)" (*ESV Study Bible*, p. 2294, note). In light of the current global uncertainties and daily news of war, terrorism, and natural disasters, how might such knowledge bolster our faith and encourage us?

---

2. The Christ-Hymn: The Son's Preeminence over the New Creation (1:18–20)

In verse 18a, the Son is called "the head of the body, the church." Paul has developed this metaphor in previous letters (1 Cor. 12:12–31; Rom. 12:4–8; compare Eph. 1:22–23; 4:4, 11–16; 5:22–23, 28–32). What truths about Christ's relationship to the church do you think the "head-body" metaphor is intended to suggest (see also Col. 1:24; 2:19)?

In 1:18b, Paul explains that the Son is "the beginning, the firstborn from the dead." The language echoes Genesis 1:1 and conveys the reality that Christ's resurrection signals the inauguration of the promised *new* creation (see Isa. 11:1–9; 65:17–25; compare Rev. 1:5; 3:14; 21:1–5a). How does the idea of the new creation fit into your current ideas of what "heaven" will be like?

"In him all the fullness of God was pleased to dwell" is Old Testament language that recalls God's presence in the tabernacle/temple (see especially

Ex. 40:34–35; 1 Kings 8:10–11; Ps. 68:16). What might be the significance of such language in terms of understanding the person of Christ?

Not only was "all the fullness of God" pleased to dwell in the Son, but God was also pleased to effect a cosmic reconciliation through the Son's death on the cross (Col. 1:20). Reconciliation implies parties that were previously estranged. What is implied about God and his creation before the cross effected reconciliation? Does the language of cosmic reconciliation suggest that everyone is or will be saved from sin? Why or why not?

3. The Christ-Hymn Applied: God Has Reconciled the Colossians to Christ (1:21–23)

In verses 21–23, Paul applies the Christ-Hymn directly to the Colossians. When the gospel arrived at Colossae, it swept the Colossians up into God's act of cosmic reconciliation through Christ. Once estranged enemies of God, those who believed the message now enjoyed peace with God. In verse 23, Paul sets forth the telltale sign that someone has truly experienced this sovereign act of reconciliation. What is the evidence that genuine salvation[1] has begun in someone's life?

Read through the following three sections on *Gospel Glimpses, Whole-Bible Connections*, and *Theological Soundings*. Then take time to consider the *Personal Implications* these sections may have for you.

▶ Gospel Glimpses

MAKING PEACE BY A CROSS. Colossians 1:20–23 teaches that there had been a cosmic estrangement between God and humanity. The estrangement included outright hostility expressed in "evil deeds" (v. 21). While such rebellion renders us ripe for God's judgment, God instead has taken the initiative to effect reconciliation. In the inscrutable wisdom of God, he made peace with his people in an unrepeatable and mysterious way. The preexistent Son took on humanity ("in his body of flesh"; v. 22) and died on a Roman instrument of torture reserved for the vilest of lawbreakers ("the blood of his cross"; v. 20). He bore our sins upon this cross, thus "making peace" between God and his people (v. 20).

THE GOAL OF CHRIST'S CROSS. The majestic Christ-Hymn, with its stunning vistas of the preeminence of the preexistent Son, could easily overshadow the stated goal of God's cosmic reconciliation effected in Christ. In verse 22, Paul states this goal: "[Christ died] in order to present you holy and blameless and above reproach before him." On the last day of history, God will complete his work in us and will present us before the judgment seat of Christ, an ordeal through which we will safely pass because of the cross of Christ.

▶ Whole-Bible Connections

CHRIST, THE WISDOM OF GOD. Colossians 1:15–20 picks up language and concepts that stem from Proverbs 8:22–31 and its later development in early Judaism. The mysterious figure of personified wisdom features in this text and its development. Wisdom was with God, acting as his agent in the creation of the world, weaving into it a moral and wise order. As the one who existed eternally with God, wisdom's experiential sagacity and resourcefulness matches God's own. Colossians claims that this literary personification of ancient Jewish literature has found its ultimate expression in the person of the eternal Son become flesh, the Lord Jesus Christ. In him are "hidden all the treasures of wisdom and knowledge" (Col. 2:3). There is therefore no need to look elsewhere for knowledge of God. Christ is the definitive and final revelation of God, giving believers all that they need in order to know God.

CHRIST, THE TEMPLE OF GOD. In the Old Testament, God dwelt in the midst of his people in the tabernacle and then later in the temple in Jerusalem. In the New Testament, God has come to dwell among his people in the person of the incarnate Son, our Lord Jesus Christ. "In him all the fullness of God was pleased to dwell" (Col. 1:19). Making a similar point, John writes concerning the eternal Son that he "became flesh and dwelt among us, and we have seen his glory" (John 1:14). Christ embodies the divine presence in the inaugurated new age of the new creation. God in Christ will dwell there with his people forever (Rev. 21:1–3, 22).

Theological Soundings

THE DEITY OF CHRIST. The phrase "firstborn of all creation" in Colossians 1:15 has created problems in the history of the church. The early heretic Arius argued that the title supported his position that Christ was a created being and that "there was a time when the Son was not." A preoccupation with the phrase apart from its immediate context, however, led to this misreading. In verse 16, the reason the Son is given this title is because "by him," "through him," and "for him" all things were created. He existed before creation. He now holds it together (v. 17). All these assertions demonstrate that the Son himself is not part of creation. He shares, rather, in the activities that elsewhere in Scripture are ascribed to God. The Son of God is fully divine (John 1:1).

THE HUMANITY OF CHRIST. Although easily overlooked because of the text's intention to exalt the preeminence of Christ over all creation as the eternal wisdom and Son of God, our Lord's humanity also shapes the passage. Christ is the "firstborn from the dead," which alludes to his humanity, as do the phrases "making peace by the blood of his cross" through "his body of flesh by his death" (Col. 1:20, 22). The eternal, divine Son took on the flesh of humanity, in what theologians call the "incarnation." He did so in order to rescue humanity from its enslavement to sin and death.

Personal Implications

Take time to reflect on the implications of Colossians 1:15–23 for your life. Consider what you have learned that might lead you to praise God, repent of sin, and trust in his gracious promises. Make notes below on the personal implications for your walk with the Lord of the (1) *Gospel Glimpses*, (2) *Whole-Bible Connections*, (3) *Theological Soundings*, and (4) this passage as a whole.

1. Gospel Glimpses

2. Whole-Bible Connections

3. Theological Soundings

4. Colossians 1:15–23

▶ As You Finish This Unit . . .

Take a moment to ask for the Lord's blessing as you continue this study. Take a moment also to review this unit, to reflect on some key things that the Lord may be teaching you—and perhaps to highlight these for review in the future.

Definition

[1] **Salvation** – Deliverance from the eternal consequences of sin. Jesus' death and resurrection purchased eternal salvation for believers (Rom. 1:16).

Week 5: Paul's Apostolic Ministry and Its Application to the Colossians

Colossians 1:24–2:5

The Place of the Passage

Paul has greeted, offered thanksgiving for, and prayed for the Colossians (1:1–14). He then celebrated Christ's supremacy over everything in the Christ-Hymn, applying Christ's cosmic redemptive work specifically to the believers at Colossae (vv. 15–23). Next, having explained his God-given apostolic charge for the nations and thus why he is writing to the Colossians (1:24–2:5), Paul will proceed to confront the false teaching directly with truth from the Christ-Hymn (2:6–23).

The Big Picture

In Colossians 1:24–2:5, Paul explains the apostolic charge given him by God to bring the message of Christ to the Gentile nations and therefore why, despite his imprisonment, he is laboring for the Colossian church and warning them against false teaching.

Reflection and Discussion

Read through the passage for this study, Colossians 1:24–2:5. Then review the questions below and write your notes on them concerning this section. (For further background, see the *ESV Study Bible*, pages 2295–2296; available online at esv.org.)

1. Paul's Apostolic Suffering and Stewardship on Behalf of the Church (1:24–25)

Paul's statement that he is "filling up what is lacking in Christ's afflictions" seems at first glance to imply that Christ's death on the cross was somehow inadequate for the salvation of the church. From the evidence in the letter itself, how do we know that this is not what Paul meant (see again 1:20–23)?

Here and elsewhere in the New Testament, we learn that God gave Paul a unique ministry in the history of the Christian movement. Paul's distinctive role as an apostle consists in suffering as "the means God uses to extend the message of the gospel to others" (*ESV Study Bible*, p. 2295 note). While suffering as a means of gospel advancement also applies to other believers in a derivative way, it applies uniquely to Paul as the apostle to the Gentiles (see Acts 9:15–16; 1 Cor. 4:9–13; 2 Cor. 1:3–11; 11:23–29; Gal. 6:17). How might this inform the statement that Paul is "filling up what is lacking in Christ's afflictions"? What is Paul able to do that Christ could not do during his earthly ministry, but that Christ was now doing from heaven through Paul on earth?

2. The Mystery of Christ (1:26–27)

According to Paul, his divine commission entails becoming a "minister" on behalf of the church, appointed to "make the word of God fully known" (Col. 1:25). This word from God consists in the message, "Christ in you, the hope of glory" (v. 27). Paul calls this message about Christ the "mystery." The word "mystery" in English typically refers to an undisclosed secret or enigma. This, however, is not what Paul intended by the word. Based on clues in the immediate context, how would you here define "mystery"?

The essence of the "mystery" that God had hidden for ages and generations, but had now revealed, is "Christ in you, the hope of glory." Unpack the meaning of this statement in your own words. (For "hope" in Colossians, see again 1:5, 23; for "glory," see 1:11 [lit. "the might of his glory"]; 3:4; compare Rom. 3:23; 5:2; 8:18, 21; 9:23).

3. The Way Paul Fulfills His Apostolic Charge, and Its Goal (1:28–29)

Reread Colossians 1:28–29. How does Paul discharge his apostolic commission "to make the word of God fully known" (v. 25)? In light of the probable esoteric nature of the false teaching, why do you think Paul repeats three times that his gospel is for "everyone"?

Read again verse 28b. What is the *goal* of Paul's apostolic proclamation? What therefore ought to be the goal of Christian proclamation today? *How* should that goal be accomplished (see again v. 28a)? *What* should be proclaimed (see again vv. 25–27)?

4. Paul's Apostolic Labor on Behalf of the Colossian Church (2:1–3)

Because Paul is the apostle for the Gentile nations, he feels a profound sense of responsibility for the fledgling church at Colossae. Therefore, despite his imprisonment and because of the encroaching false teaching, Paul labors and "struggles" in prayer for the Colossian church. According to verses 1–3, what is the goal of this "struggling"?

Read 4:12, concerning Epaphras's "struggle" for the Colossians. Besides writing letters, proclaiming the gospel, and contending against false teachings, in what other kind of ministry does Paul "struggle" on behalf of the church at Colossae? (See again 1:9–14 as a model example of this ministry.)

5. The Goal of Paul's Instruction: "Let No One Deceive You" (2:4–5)

Against the false teaching, which claimed to be the true path to divine wisdom (see 2:23), Paul asserts that in Christ "are hidden all the treasures of wisdom and knowledge" (v. 3). All true knowledge and wisdom are found in Christ and available to *all* his people. According to verse 4, why has Paul stressed this truth? What made the false teaching tempting? Had the church as a whole succumbed to the false teaching (v. 5)?

_____

_____

_____

_____

_____

_____

_____

Read through the following three sections on *Gospel Glimpses*, *Whole-Bible Connections*, and *Theological Soundings*. Then take time to consider the *Personal Implications* these sections may have for you.

▶ Gospel Glimpses

CHRIST, THE MYSTERY. Hidden by God for ages and generations, Christ has, at the turn of the ages, been revealed as the centerpiece of God's plan for the cosmic reconciliation of all things. He is the key that unlocks the eternal divine plan for human history. This unprecedented divine revelation—like the previous biblical "mysteries" before it (see, e.g., Dan. 2:17–49)—requires divinely provided interpretation to be understood. Paul, as God's appointed ambassador, is charged to interpret the mystery of Christ for the Gentile peoples of the earth (1:1, 25, 28–29). When we learn about Christ, we discover the key that unlocks human history and therefore the reason for our existence.

"CHRIST IN YOU, THE HOPE OF GLORY." By virtue of their union with Israel's Messiah ("Christ"), Gentile believers enjoy the unshakeable hope that they will share in the glory of God. Humanity lost this glory in Adam's rebellion (Genesis 3; see Rom. 3:23), but God's plan of cosmic renewal includes the restoration of humanity as the faithful image of God, clothed in glory (Col. 3:4, 9–10; Rom. 5:2; 8:17–21, 29–30). Christ's powerful indwelling presence ensures and assures us that this inner transformation is taking place and will be completed on the day of his triumphant return (Col. 3:4, 9–10; Phil. 1:6).

Whole-Bible Connections

GENTILE INCLUSION INTO THE PEOPLE OF GOD. Christians today take for granted that the gospel is for everyone irrespective of ethnic origin. But when the gospel first burst upon the scene of history, such a concept was new and even scandalous. The Jewish nation of Israel had been the people of God for centuries. The rest of the peoples of the world were outside the covenants of God and considered unclean, sinful, and cut off from God (compare Matt. 18:17; Gal. 1:15; Eph. 2:11–12). However, the Old Testament promised that one day the Gentiles would seek God and become full members of his people (e.g., Isa. 2:2–3; 19:23–25; Zech. 2:10–11). These promises found their fulfillment in Christ. Consequently, Paul was charged with making Christ known "to [God's] saints . . . among the Gentiles" (Col. 1:26b–27).

THE HIDDENNESS OF CHRIST IN THE OLD TESTAMENT EPOCH. The idea that Christ appears in the Old Testament is popular but must be properly understood. Colossians 1:26–27 teaches that God had hid Christ away from human purview until the time of eschatological fulfillment. Therefore, strictly speaking, Christ as the climax of divine disclosure was not revealed until his incarnation and birth (compare Gal. 4:4). It is more accurate to say that there are *prefigurations* and *promises* of Christ in the Old Testament, which point forward to the day when the Father would finally unveil his Son.

Theological Soundings

SUFFERING. Paul played a unique role in redemptive history by virtue of his divine commission as apostle to the Gentiles. As Christ suffered on behalf of his people to purchase salvation for them, so Paul suffered to bring the salvation purchased by Christ to those who had not yet heard the message. This is what "is lacking" in the afflictions of Christ (Col. 1:24). Paul's suffering was unique to his apostolic vocation (Acts 9:15–16; 1 Cor. 4:9–13; 2 Cor. 11:23–29). After the pattern of his Lord, Paul's suffering functioned to bring salvation to others. In a derivative way, all believers partake in such redemptive suffering. None of it is wasted for those who trust Christ, and all of it serves ultimately to advance God's purposes of redemption for the world (Rom. 8:18, 28; 2 Cor. 4:17).

CHRIST, STOREHOUSE OF DIVINE WISDOM. The book of Proverbs teaches that God is the fountainhead of all wisdom and knowledge. He has woven order into creation, including moral order. Colossians 2:3 teaches that what was true of God in the Old Testament can now also be said to be true of the Son. "In [him] are hidden all the treasures of wisdom and knowledge" (2:3). The Son makes these treasures available to his people through Scripture and prayer in the Spirit (1:9; 3:16).

► Personal Implications

Take time to reflect on the implications of Colossians 1:24–2:5 for your life. Consider what you have learned that might lead you to praise God, repent of sin, and trust in his gracious promises. Make notes below on the personal implications for your walk with the Lord of the (1) *Gospel Glimpses*, (2) *Whole-Bible Connections*, (3) *Theological Soundings*, and (4) this passage as a whole.

1. Gospel Glimpses

2. Whole-Bible Connections

3. Theological Soundings

4. Colossians 1:24–2:5

As You Finish This Unit . . .

Take a moment to ask for the Lord's blessing as you continue this study. Take a moment also to review this unit, to reflect on some key things that the Lord may be teaching you—and perhaps to highlight these for review in the future.

WEEK 6: PAUL CONFRONTS THE FALSE TEACHING

Colossians 2:6–23

▲

The Place of the Passage

Having completed the introduction of his letter, highlighting the preeminence of Christ and explaining his own apostolic role in the divine plan for history (Col. 1:1–2:5), Paul now turns to the heart of the matter to confront directly the false teaching on offer at Colossae (2:6–23).

The Big Picture

The Colossian faithful are to reject the false teaching being offered by some people in their midst, because in Christ they have all they need for salvation and for their ongoing life with God.

Read through Colossians 2:6–23. Then review the questions below and write your notes on them concerning this section. (For further background, see the *ESV Study Bible*, pages 2296–2298; available online at esv.org.)

1. "Walk in Him": Paul's Programmatic Statement (2:6–7)

Epaphras had faithfully handed on to the Colossians the apostolic gospel that Jesus is Lord. The Colossians had received this message and had been firmly rooted in it. Now, as a first strike against the heresy, Paul urges them to continue to "walk in [Christ]." What do you think this might mean? And how might "abounding in thanksgiving" function as an integral way of ensuring that the Colossians remain faithful to Christ as Lord in every area of life?

2. "See to It That No One Takes You Captive": The Warning against the Heresy (2:8)

Since the believers were to continue to live in union with Christ and to work out his lordship in their lives, Paul warns them against the heresy. This "philosophy" was not in accordance with Christ but originated merely in "human tradition." Paul then implies, however, that in reality its origin is even deeper and more sinister than this ("according to the elemental spirits of the world"). What do you think he means?

3. Fullness of Salvation in Christ: Four Reasons to Resist the Empty Heresy (2:9–15)

In verses 9–10, Paul offers his first reason for why the Colossians should not be enamored with the heresy. This is because, while it apparently promised a deeper experience of the presence of God, it could not deliver. Picking up earlier language from the Christ-Hymn at 1:19, how does Paul counteract this empty claim?

In verses 11–12a, Paul provides a second reason for why his audience must resist the heresy. It is because "in Christ" they were "circumcised" spiritually. While it remains a debated component of the overall scenario, it is agreed that there was a significant Jewish strain to the false teaching (see 2:16). The heresy, therefore, may have prescribed circumcision to be pleasing to God. Based on the clues embedded in the context, what might Paul have meant by spiritual circumcision?

In verses 12b–14, Paul supplies a third reason for why his audience must withstand the heresy. God has raised them from (spiritual) death by virtue of their union with the resurrected Christ. List the two achievements of God in Christ that preceded and made this resurrection possible (vv. 13b–14). Then, reflect on their significance.

In verse 15, Paul supplies a fourth reason to resist the false teaching. There is abundant evidence from the ancient Greco-Roman world that people lived in fear of spirits and the demonic realm and were often preoccupied with how to appease them. The heresy apparently offered a way to appease these "rulers and authorities" or claimed to provide protection against them. How does Paul's teaching in verse 15 surpass what the heresy offered?

4. Let No One Condemn You: Old Covenant Regulations and Visionary Experience (2:16–19)

Because of the four reasons provided in verses 9–15, Paul draws the conclusion that the Colossian faithful should let no adherent of the heresy "pass judgment" or "disqualify" them. According to verse 19, what is the fundamental problem with the false teachers, resulting in their vain and arrogant spirit?

5. Dead with Christ to Demonic Powers, the Fallen Age, and Man-Made Religion (2:20–23)

The Colossians still lived in this fallen age ("the world"), but they had died in Christ's death to the powers that held sway over it (compare Gal. 1:4). In your own words, describe the characteristics of the false teaching as depicted in these verses. Then reflect upon why it may have been attractive to the Colossian disciples.

Read through the following three sections on *Gospel Glimpses, Whole-Bible Connections*, and *Theological Soundings*. Then take time to consider the *Personal Implications* these sections may have for you.

Gospel Glimpses

UNION WITH CHRIST. A central pillar of Paul's thought surfaces in Colossians 2:6–15 with his frequent use of the phrases "in him" or "with him" (i.e., Christ) at key points in the argument. Paul understands that believers enjoy an unbreakable and everlasting spiritual union with Christ, which began the moment they first placed their trust in him. Because of this union, what is true of Christ becomes derivatively true of his followers. He is filled with God's fullness, and by virtue of their union with him they are also filled (2:9–10). In his "circumcision" (i.e., death), they are "circumcised" (v. 11). In his burial and resurrection, they have undergone burial and new life (vv. 12–13). In his decisive defeat of the demonic powers, they experience victory (vv. 10, 15, 20). The Head-Body metaphor in the letter is another way of describing this relationship (1:18, 24; 2:19; compare Eph. 1:22–23; 4:15–16; 5:23; 1 Cor. 12:12–31).

DYING AND RISING WITH CHRIST. Paul teaches that believers—by virtue of their union with Christ—have died and been raised in Christ's death and resurrection. This means that we no longer belong to the fallen world and present evil age. Christ lives with God, free from the sin and death that characterize this age. By virtue of his work for us on the cross and our union with him, the world's powers likewise no longer enslave us. We are free from the penalty and power of sin. This includes freedom from the "elemental spirits of the world," the Satanic forces who oppress the fallen world and devise false worldviews to lead it astray.

Whole-Bible Connections

THE TEMPLE OF GOD OF THE NEW AGE. Picking up language from Colossians 1:19, which echoes Old Testament language concerning God's presence in the temple at Zion, Paul writes that in the dawning of the new age in Christ, the divine presence is now found in a person, not in a building. "In [Christ] the whole fullness of deity dwells bodily" (2:9). This stunning revelation develops even further, however, as disciples discover that by union with Christ they have become extensions of this temple (2:10). They are the

47

locus of the divine presence in the world, both individually and corporately (1 Cor. 3:16–17; 6:19).

THE CIRCUMCISION OF CHRIST. The Old Testament prescribed circumcision for every male member of Abraham's family as a sign of covenant membership and as a symbol of consecration to God (Gen. 17:9–14). Women were included by virtue of their links with men. According to Paul, Christ's death has provided all his people with a spiritual circumcision that marks them out as members of the new covenant people of God. The symbol has given way to the promised reality, enabling Christians to live out a true consecration to God (Deut. 30:6).

Theological Soundings

JESUS, THE LORD. The fundamental confession of devotion in the early church was, "Jesus is Lord" (see Col. 2:6; Rom. 10:9; 1 Cor. 8:6; 12:3; 2 Cor. 4:5; Phil. 2:11). The Greek word for "Lord" is the same used in the Greek Old Testament to translate the personal name of God, YHWH. The implications of this for the identity of Jesus Christ were unmistakable. At the same time, however, the New Testament documents are equally insistent that there is only one God. This "christological monotheism" characterizes the entire New Testament witness about Jesus. It pervades Paul's letter to the Colossians.

FALSE WORLDVIEWS AND THE DEMONIC POWERS. While it is considered politically incorrect in our postmodern world for one worldview to denounce others as false, the Bible does not hesitate to do so. From Paul's point of view, any worldview that led people away from the one true God as revealed in the gospel of Christ was a man-made creation, whose source was ultimately demonic. Such demonic powers held sway over the world and enslaved it through lies and through playing upon fears. In love, Christian Scripture offers an ultimate worldview and asserts that it is the only true one. Christians must take care not to succumb too quickly to the postmodern clamor for tolerance, before they have thought through Scripture's witness and how it might apply to the postmodern context.

Personal Implications

Take time to reflect on the implications of Colossians 2:6–23 for your life. Consider what you have learned that might lead you to praise God, repent of sin, and trust in his gracious promises. Make notes below on the personal implications for your walk with the Lord of the (1) *Gospel Glimpses*, (2) *Whole-Bible Connections*, (3) *Theological Soundings*, and (4) this passage as a whole.

1. Gospel Glimpses

2. Whole-Bible Connections

3. Theological Soundings

4. Colossians 2:6–23

> ### As You Finish This Unit . . .

Take a moment to ask for the Lord's blessing as you continue this study. Take a moment also to review this unit, to reflect on some key things that the Lord may be teaching you—and perhaps to highlight these for review in the future.

Week 7: Exhortation: Seek Instead the Things of Christ Above

Colossians 3:1–17

The Place of the Passage

Having confronted the false teaching directly, exposing it as a bankrupt system that denigrates Christ's preeminence and sufficiency (Col. 2:6–23), Paul draws an inference and provides the only reasonable alternative. The Colossians must instead focus on Christ alone and become who they are in him (3:1–4). They must strip off, like filthy ruined clothes, the practices that belong to the fallen old humanity to which they once belonged (3:5–11). They can do so because, in Christ, this old humanity has been stripped off. They have donned instead, like a fresh garment, the new humanity of the new creation in Christ. They therefore must become who they are in Christ. Consequently, they must become marked by the practices of this new humanity, putting on above all the cardinal virtue of love (3:12–17).

The Big Picture

In Colossians 3:1–17, Paul exhorts the Colossian disciples to become who they are in Christ, the last Adam, whose perfect image and character serve as prototype and pattern for their own renewal as image-bearers of God.

▶ Reflection and Discussion

Read through the passage for this study. Then review the questions below and write your notes on them concerning this section of the letter. (For further background, see the *ESV Study Bible*, pages 2298–2299; available online at esv.org.)

1. Reshaping Reality: The Resurrected and Reigning Christ (3:1–4)

The Colossian Christians had died and been raised together with Christ (vv. 1, 3). They were now hidden away with Christ in God (v. 3). At Christ's return on the last day of history, they would be revealed with him, clothed in glory (v. 4; see 1:27). What is true of Christ becomes derivatively true of those united to him by faith. How does Paul use these theological realities to ground his exhortation to "seek the things above"? What do you think it means to "seek the things above"?

The language of the heavenly things "above" and the things that are "on earth" is not intended to imply that the immaterial world (e.g., the soul) is good, whereas the physical world (e.g., the body or food or sex) is evil. Such a notion is indebted more to ancient Greek philosophy than to Christian Scripture, which teaches that everything God created was "good" (Genesis 1:31). Instead, this is a spatial way of talking about two ages: the present fallen age dominated by sin and demonic powers (the corrupted old creation), and the future age of the kingdom of God (the incorruptible new creation). According to this text, where do believers live? To what age do they belong? How did Paul expect this to impact their life?

2. Strip Off the Fallen Old Humanity, with Its Vices (3:5–11)

According to Colossians 3:5–11, what must a disciple do to maintain kingdom focus? Why do you think Paul chose such strong language as "putting [these things] to death" (v. 5)?

In verses 9b–10, Paul offers a reason for why disciples must put away the vices listed in verses 5–9a. The reason is that they have stripped off the "old self" (literally, the "old man" or "old humanity") and have donned as a new garment the "new self" (literally, the "new man" or "new humanity"). This "new self" in Christ is in the process of being renewed into the image of God (see Gen. 1:26–27). Reflect on Paul's logic at this point. *Why* should this new reality mean that they must no longer participate in the vices that mark the fallen world and its humanity?

3. Put On the New Humanity, with Its Virtues (3:12–17)

Paul draws another inference at Colossians 3:12. Because they have "put on the new self" in Christ, the church is to "put on" the virtues that correspond to the new humanity that God is re-creating in Christ. List, and then take some time to reflect upon, the virtues mentioned in verses 12–17.

As elsewhere in Paul's letters, "love" holds pride of place as the cardinal virtue that summarizes what God requires of his new covenant people (Col. 3:14; see Rom. 13:8–10; 1 Cor. 13:1–13; Gal. 5:6, 13–14, 22a; Eph. 5:1–2). Reflect upon how contemporary society defines love, and then attempt to define love from the Scripture texts mentioned above (see also John 3:16; 13:34–35; 1 John 4:10–11).

Read through the following three sections on *Gospel Glimpses*, *Whole-Bible Connections*, and *Theological Soundings*. Then take time to consider the *Personal Implications* these sections may have for you.

▶ Gospel Glimpses

SAVED FROM THE WRATH OF GOD. While not a major theme of Colossians, the subject of deliverance from the wrath of God and final judgment emerges at 3:6. Because of its rebellion against God, fallen humanity is destined for God's righteous judgment at the end of history. Christians once belonged to this fallen humanity (3:7), but God stooped down and rescued us in his mercy when we "received Christ Jesus the Lord" (2:6). Jesus is our Savior, who "delivers us from the wrath to come" (1 Thess. 1:10).

THE GOSPEL AND ETHNICITY. Through the gospel of Christ, God is creating a new humanity. The ethnic, social, and economic divisions that characterize fallen humanity no longer define the people whom God is re-creating in Christ. Instead, Christ "is all, and in all" (3:11). While we do not cease to be Ethiopian or Korean or French or Brazilian when Christ saves us, these ethnic badges no longer function to identify who we ultimately are. Instead, Christ defines the new humanity of the dawning new creation.

▶ Whole-Bible Connections

THE IMAGE OF GOD AND CHRIST. An entire epic story stands behind Paul's thought in his letter to the Colossians and emerges at key points in the letter. One glimpse of the story shines through at 3:9–10, where Paul alludes to Genesis 1:26–27. In the beginning, God created humanity in his image to rule the world as his wise and benevolent stewards. Their task was to establish the kingdom of God on the earth through their loyal service. However, according to Genesis 3 Adam and Eve rebelled against their Creator-King, plunging the world into sin and death. Therefore, God sent his Son to take on the world's rebellion and conquer it. He did so in his death and resurrection. He now pours out his Spirit upon his people, re-creating them as true image-bearers, in and through whom God will fulfill his Genesis 1 intentions for creation. Christ as the definitive image of God serves as the prototype for this new humanity (Col. 1:15; compare Rom. 5:12–21; 8:29; 1 Cor. 15:20–22, 42–49; 2 Cor. 4:4).

PSALM 110 AND CHRIST'S ENTHRONEMENT. In the phrase "seated at the right hand of God," Paul at Colossians 3:1 alludes to the Old Testament text most often quoted in the New Testament, Psalm 110:1. A glance at the original context reveals that the text is a royal psalm concerning an ideal Davidic king. This king is enthroned at the right hand of God and is vested with full authority to conquer, judge, and rule all those who are the sworn enemies of God and his people. Paul understands this psalm to find its ultimate fulfillment in Christ. He is the ultimate Son of David. Enthroned with divine authority, Christ now establishes God's rule on the earth, having defeated at the cross the demonic powers that stand in his way (Col. 2:15).

> **Theological Soundings**

SANCTIFICATION. While Scripture teaches that we were declared holy when we first received Christ (see 1 Cor. 6:11), it also teaches that we are to actively and daily pursue growth in personal holiness. Paul himself calls the Colossians "God's chosen ones, holy and beloved" (Col. 3:12). However, he then immediately exhorts them to "put on" the new humanity with all its accompanying virtues (3:12b–17). Our assurance, in what is sometimes a discouraging process, is "Christ in you, the hope of glory" (1:27). Christ is working in us by his Spirit, ensuring that we are being renewed as image-bearers of God (3:9–10). What he has begun in us he has promised to complete (Phil. 1:6).

THE WORD OF CHRIST. God uses means to grow us in holiness. One of the central means God uses to renew us into the image of God is Scripture. In 3:16, Paul urges the Colossians to "let the word of Christ dwell" among them richly. The message of Christ was to inhabit the center of the community's life and worship. It was to be allowed to penetrate deeply and richly, thus producing a flourishing, Christ-following community. It was to be taught and sung. Today, if we are to grow in holiness, we also must let Scripture inhabit the center of our Christian community's life and worship.

Personal Implications

Take time to reflect on the implications of Colossians 3:1–17 for your life. Consider what you have learned that might lead you to praise God, repent of sin, and trust in his gracious promises. Make notes below on the personal implications for your walk with the Lord of the (1) *Gospel Glimpses*, (2) *Whole-Bible Connections*, (3) *Theological Soundings*, and (4) this passage as a whole.

1. Gospel Glimpses

2. Whole-Bible Connections

3. Theological Soundings

4. Colossians 3:1–17

As You Finish This Unit . . .

Take a moment to ask for the Lord's blessing as you continue this study. Take a moment also to review this unit, to reflect on some key things that the Lord may be teaching you—and perhaps to highlight these for review in the future.

Week 8: Instructions for Relationships both inside and outside the Faith

Colossians 3:18–4:6

The Place of the Passage

Colossians 3:18–4:6 concludes the body of the letter. Paul has confronted the false teaching (2:6–23). He then followed this up with an exhortation to focus fully on the resurrected and reigning Christ (3:1–17). Now, in the text to be studied this week, the apostle provides instruction for the believers' household relationships "in the Lord" (3:18–4:1). He will then turn to give instruction for their relationships with those outside and unfamiliar with the faith (4:2–6).

The Big Picture

In Colossians 3:18–4:6, Paul provides specific instructions for believers' relationships with members of their own household (3:18–4:1) as well as with those outside and unfamiliar with the Christian faith (4:2–6).

Reflection and Discussion

Read the text for this week's study. Then review the following questions and write your notes on them concerning this section. (For further background, see the *ESV Study Bible*, pages 2299–2300; available online at esv.org.)

1. Wives and Husbands (3:18–19)

In Paul's Greco-Roman world, a husband and father was the *paterfamilias*, or male head of his household. Though liable to becoming abusive in that role, according to Roman law he nevertheless held absolute power over the rest of his house. At first glance, it appears that Paul simply mirrors the highest cultural ideals for marriage within this patriarchal framework. Yet, while there is little doubt that Paul was influenced by his own culture, the picture is not as simple as this, for Paul states that his instruction to wives is "fitting in the Lord." This indicates that Paul's instruction reaches beyond Greco-Roman culture to Christ himself (compare Eph. 5:22–33). How might Paul's instruction to the husband (Col. 3:19) have transformed the *paterfamilias* role?

2. Children and Parents (3:20–21)

As in the previous two verses, Paul addresses the people with less authority in the relationship first. He thereby treats them as morally responsible agents and bestows upon them the dignity of personhood and value. Echoing Old Testament instruction (Ex. 20:12), Paul instructs that children are to honor parental authority. What reason does Paul give as motivation for this obedience? Yet how does Paul's instruction to "fathers" (and mothers) seek to ensure that the child's compliance is not abused?

3. Slaves and Masters (3:22–4:1)

In the Greco-Roman world, most households of some means possessed male and female slaves. Legally and economically, slaves were regarded as property and masters had complete authority over them. Repulsive to modern Western sensibilities as this seems, in what ways might "Christ, the Lord" have transformed this ancient relationship? Although limited in applicability, how might Paul's instruction apply to employer/employee relationships today?

----

4. Exhortation to Missional Prayer (4:2–4)

While Paul begins verse 2 with a general exhortation to cultivate a prayer life (marked by "thanksgiving"; compare 1:3, 12; 2:7; 3:17), it quickly develops into an appeal for his apostolic ministry. The imprisoned apostle requests "door-opening" prayer so that "the mystery of Christ" may be shared with more and more people (1:25–27; for historical background, see Acts 28:16–31). Obviously, since Paul is now in eternity with Christ, the church is no longer required to pray for his ministry, yet what are the applicable principles behind these verses?

----

5. Walk Wisely to Attract Outsiders (4:5–6)

While the Colossians are to be wary of the false teachers among them, Paul does not mean that they should disengage from relationship with citizens of Colossae who are unfamiliar with the Christian faith. Indeed, Paul's instruction encourages wise and winsome witness that commends the faith to outsiders.

WEEK 8: INSTRUCTIONS FOR RELATIONSHIPS

Why do you think Paul injects a note of urgency with the phrase, "making the best use of the time"? What do you think it might mean for their speech to be "seasoned with salt"?

_____

_____

_____

_____

_____

_____

Read through the following three sections on *Gospel Glimpses, Whole-Bible Connections*, and *Theological Soundings*. Then take time to consider the *Personal Implications* these sections may have for you.

> ## Gospel Glimpses

THE GOSPEL AND CULTURE. Colossians 3:18–4:1 has attracted its share of criticism in an increasingly post-Christian and postmodern West. Critics disparage Paul as a misogynist (a man who hates women) or as a racist who, if alive today, would have upheld the (now abolished) eighteenth- and nineteenth-century slave trades. Both of these caricatures fail to understand Paul. Paul was not a social revolutionary but an apostle of the gospel. He knew that the way to change less-than-ideal elements of the prevailing culture was not to attempt to enforce God's ways politically (which, for the numerically insignificant house churches in Paul's day, would have been impossible anyway). Rather, genuine and lasting change would come through inward transformation of individual hearts. The gospel provided this with its gift of the Spirit and the new heart. Like invisible leaven inside a batch of dough, the gospel works quietly within, bringing about healing and transformed lives. It re-creates people who seek to cultivate God's just and benevolent ways. Often overlooked, the abolition of slavery in the nineteenth century arose due in no small measure to concerned Christians laboring tirelessly on behalf of the oppressed. Women's rights flowered in the twentieth century in the West because of the strongly held democratic ideal of equality. This is a concept that ultimately originates from Genesis 1 and its teaching that every individual is inherently valuable because of being made in the image of God.

Whole-Bible Connections

THE INHERITANCE. The word "inheritance" in Colossians 3:24 resonates with deep Old Testament overtones, providing a window into the church's future hope. Paul grounds his exhortation to household slaves, who normally would not inherit anything from the *paterfamilias* when he died, with the promise that they will "receive the inheritance" as a recompense for faithful service to Christ. The word "inheritance" first occurred in 1:12–13 and refers there to the everlasting kingdom of God. In the Old Testament, "inheritance" referred to the allotments of property given to each family of the 12 tribes of Israel within the Promised Land. In the New Testament, such language is picked up and its referent extended to encompass the entire world of the promised new creation. From this perspective, the Promised Land in the Old Testament offers a prefiguration of the believer's ultimate future inheritance.

Theological Soundings

PRAYER. Paul urges Christians to cultivate a regular prayer life (Col. 4:2). Sweet communion with our heavenly Father is at the very heart of what Christ purchased for us with his own blood. He died to restore intimate relationship between God and his people. Some view prayer as a duty rather than a delight. Prayer *is* commanded of us, of course, and so it is a "duty" in one sense. But it is sort of like being commanded to eat a large portion of your favorite dessert. Paul commands us to pursue what our soul longs for: an ever-deepening relationship with the soul-satisfying God. No one or nothing else will satisfy. Yet people waste years searching in vain for what will quench their insatiable thirst. Rather, let us relentlessly labor to enjoy God's presence in soul-satisfying communion with him.

Personal Implications

Take time to reflect on the implications of Colossians 3:18–4:6 for your life. Consider what you have learned that might lead you to praise God, repent of sin, and trust in his gracious promises. Make notes below on the personal implications for your walk with the Lord of the (1) *Gospel Glimpses*, (2) *Whole-Bible Connections*, (3) *Theological Soundings*, and (4) this passage as a whole.

1. Gospel Glimpses

2. Whole-Bible Connections

3. Theological Soundings

4. Colossians 3:18–4:6

As You Finish This Unit . . .

Take a moment to ask for the Lord's blessing as you continue this study. Take a moment also to review this unit, to reflect on some key things that the Lord may be teaching you—and perhaps to highlight for review in the future.

WEEK 9: THE LETTER'S CONCLUSION: GREETINGS AND FINAL INSTRUCTIONS

Colossians 4:7–18

The Place of the Passage

Most written letters, both of ancient times and today, have some standard structural elements to them. Paul's letter to the Colossians is no different. Having introduced himself and Timothy, he greeted the Colossian faithful, thanking God for them and then praying for them (Col. 1:1–14). He then proceeded immediately to the body of the letter. Here the apostle exalted the preeminence of the Son in the Christ-Hymn, unleashing it as ammunition against the lethal false teaching on offer at Colossae (1:15–2:23). In light of this strong refutation, Paul then exhorted the assembly to focus fully on the resurrected and reigning Christ above and to live in light of his reality (3:1–4:6). Finally, having completed his argument and exhortation, Paul concludes the letter, passing on greetings and final instructions (4:7–18).

The Big Picture

In Colossians 4:7–18, Paul concludes his letter. He passes on greetings from six coworkers and provides final instructions to ensure that the Colossian and Laodicean churches will remain steadfast in the faith.

> **Reflection and Discussion**

Read through the text for this study. Then review the questions below and write your notes on them. (For further background, see the *ESV Study Bible*, page 2300; available online at esv.org.)

1. Tychicus, Letter Carrier and Apostolic Delegate, with Onesimus (4:7–9)

With no postal service available, Paul sent Tychicus as the bearer of the letter. (Tychicus probably also carried the letters to the Ephesians and to Philemon; see Eph. 6:21–22.) Tychicus had been a faithful colleague for some time (Acts 20:4; compare Titus 3:12; 2 Tim. 4:12). He would read the letter aloud to the assembled house church, filling out its instruction as questions arose. Paul wanted to ensure that the Colossians gave Tychicus a respectful hearing, and this is why he provided Tychicus with the three honorific titles. What are the *explicit* reasons that Paul gives for sending Tychicus (compare Col. 2:1–2a)?

Intentionally mentioned at the end of verses 7–9 for rhetorical effect, Onesimus is the runaway slave turned faithful Christian, with whom Paul's companion letter to Philemon is concerned. (See the next two weeks of study in this guide.) How might Paul's descriptors of Onesimus in verse 9 prepare the way for a sympathetic hearing of Paul's letter by Philemon, Onesimus's slighted owner?

2. Greetings: Three Jewish Christian Coworkers with Paul (4:10–11)

The theological and temporal priority in God's plan of redemption was that the gospel must first go to his covenant people, Israel (the "Jews"; Matt. 10:5–6; 15:24; Acts 13:46–47; 18:5–6; 28:28; Rom. 1:16). Initially a Messianic movement within Judaism, the Christian faith quickly spread and became predominantly Gentile in its adherents. Jewish resistance arose against the movement from its birth, however, and Jewish opponents harassed Paul throughout his missionary journeys (e.g., Acts 9:19b–25; 13:44–45; 14:1–7, 19; 17:1–5; 18:5–6, 12; 20:19; 21:27–32; 23:12–15). Against this background, how might faithful *Jewish* Christian colleagues be a "comfort" to the imprisoned apostle?

3. Greetings: Three Gentile Christian Coworkers with Paul (4:12–14)

God called Paul to be the apostle to the Gentiles (Acts 9:15; Gal. 2:8). The Lord used him mightily to plant churches throughout the Roman empire. Over time, Gentile converts matured enough so that some of them were so dedicated to the cause that Paul enlisted them to be his colleagues. Epaphras was one of these colleagues. Based on Colossians 1:7–8; 4:12–13 and Philemon 23, piece together Epaphras's role and significance.

4. Instructions concerning the Church at Laodicea (4:15–16)

Paul here gives final instructions to the church at Colossae. He wishes to ensure that the churches at both Colossae and Laodicea remain firm in the faith (compare Col. 2:1). List the actions that Paul commands the Colossian church to take. How might each action help to ensure that both churches will continue to stand firm?

----

5. Instruction for Archippus (4:17)

Paul gives specific instructions to a man named Archippus. Apparently, Archippus is a leader in the house church at Colossae (see Philemon 2). How might this instruction to Archippus help to ensure that the Colossian church will remain firm in the faith?

----

6. Paul's Personal Authentication of the Letter and Final Blessing (4:18)

The first sentence within this verse seems a bit strange at first glance. What do you think the apostle is doing here? Second, why do you think Paul asks the Colossians to remember him in his imprisonment? What does he hope to elicit? Finally, how do you think the church might obtain the "grace" that Paul seeks for them in his blessing? What role may the letter itself play as a means to this grace?

Read through the following three sections on *Gospel Glimpses, Whole-Bible Connections,* and *Theological Soundings.* Then take time to consider the *Personal Implications* these sections may have for you.

Gospel Glimpses

TEAM PAUL. Although Paul is justly renowned for his apostolic ministry, including the 13 letters in the New Testament that are attributed to him, Paul could never have accomplished the ministry he did without help. The text for this week is just 12 short verses, yet it mentions no fewer than eight colleagues (10, if Nympha and Archippus are included). These colleagues served as letter couriers, delegates, church planters, pastors, and hosts of house churches. They were also faithful friends and prayer partners. The church must never forget that gospel ministry is always a team effort.

WRESTLING WITH THE GOSPEL. The New Testament provides glimpses elsewhere of most of the colleagues mentioned in 4:7–18. They show real and ordinary people wrestling with the gospel in their own lives. Onesimus, for example, is a runaway slave who has become a Christian. Consequently, he is returning to his legal master because, in God's sight, this is the right thing to do. He is, however, unsure as to what the outcome will be. Mark, a previous colleague of Paul, deserted the apostle at one point on a past missionary journey (Acts 15:36–40). Years later, the gospel has worked in Mark's life (as well as in Paul's!); the two have agreed to join hands together again in ministry. Demas will wrestle with the gospel and its claim on his life. He will, however, eventually reject the gospel for himself. He eventually abandons Paul to run after the world (2 Tim. 4:10).

Whole-Bible Connections

GENTILE INCLUSION INTO THE PEOPLE OF GOD. The list of Paul's colleagues in Colossians 4:7–18 includes seven Gentiles. The church today easily overlooks the significance of Gentile inclusion into the people of God at the beginning of the early Christian movement. But it was the arrival of Jesus as Israel's Messiah that signaled the age of fulfillment and that therefore it was time to gather the Gentiles into the fold, as the Scriptures had foretold (e.g., Gen. 12:3; Isa. 2:2–3; 19:23–25; 49:6; 56:3–8; 60:1–9; Zech. 2:10–11).

THE KINGDOM OF GOD. Paul mentions the "kingdom of God" at Colossians 4:11, but he does not elaborate. Yet the theme of kingdom stands at the heart of the biblical epic. In the beginning, the Creator-King's original intention was

71

to establish his heavenly rule on earth through a loyal and flourishing human community. Heaven and earth would intersect, and the King's glory would fill the earth as the waters cover the sea (Isa. 11:9; Hab. 2:14). However, God's image-bearers rebelled against his kingship. The rest of the epic concerns how God is working to fulfill his original intention for creation. With the arrival of Jesus, God's kingdom has been decisively established upon the earth forever (Mark 1:15). When Christ returns at the end of history, God will realize his original kingdom intention for creation. Until then, Paul labored tirelessly, as did his colleagues, "for the kingdom of God."

Theological Soundings

GOD'S SOVEREIGNTY AND PAUL'S IMPRISONMENT. Paul was in prison when he wrote his letter to the Colossians. Prohibited from traveling to visit existing churches or to plant new ones, Paul would have been deeply concerned about the progress of the gospel (compare 2 Cor. 11:28). However, what looked to be gospel-inhibiting circumstances produced more gospel advancement than if Paul had not ended up in prison (compare Phil. 1:12). During his imprisonment, Paul wrote the letters to the Colossians, Ephesians, Philippians, and Philemon. Eventually recognized as Scripture by the church, these four letters have proved to be priceless resources of instruction and encouragement for millions of Christians over the last 2,000 years. Yet these letters came about only because God wisely and sovereignly ordained that Paul be imprisoned for his faithfulness.

SCRIPTURE. Cosmologists today are left to ponder what a glimpse of the formation of galaxies at the dawn of the universe would have revealed. In a similar way, biblical scholars ponder what a glimpse back into the dawn of the early Christian movement would reveal about the formation of the earliest Christian writings. They receive a tantalizing peek in Colossians 4:16. Two letters of Paul, one possibly now lost (the so-called "letter to the Laodiceans"; some have speculated that it could be Ephesians), were to be read aloud at their respective destinations. They were then to be copied and shared with the other church. Not yet universally recognized as Scripture, these two letters were nevertheless understood to carry apostolic authority and to be accurate in their communication of the gospel. The New Testament was in process of formation.

Personal Implications

Take time to reflect on the implications of Colossians 4:7–18 for your life. Consider what you have learned that might lead you to praise God, repent of sin, and trust in his gracious promises. Make notes below on the personal implications for

your walk with the Lord of the (1) *Gospel Glimpses*, (2) *Whole-Bible Connections*, (3) *Theological Soundings*, and (4) this passage as a whole.

1. Gospel Glimpses

2. Whole-Bible Connections

3. Theological Soundings

4. Colossians 4:7–18

As You Finish This Unit . . .

Take a moment to ask for the Lord's blessing as you finish this study of Colossians. Take a moment also to review this unit, to reflect on some key things that the Lord may be teaching you—and perhaps to highlight for review in the future.

WEEK 10: PAUL'S GREETING OF AND THANKSGIVING FOR PHILEMON

Philemon 1–7

The Place of the Passage

In his letter to Philemon, Paul is attempting to navigate an extremely sensitive situation. Onesimus, a runaway slave, has found the imprisoned Paul in Rome. Onesimus has fled from his master Philemon, a Gentile Christian and house church leader in Colossae. (Onesimus apparently has also stolen money or property; see vv. 18–19.) During his time with Paul, Onesimus has converted to the Christian faith and has become useful to the apostle in ministry. Paul knows, however, that estrangement between Christian brothers is contrary to the gospel, since God himself had effected reconciliation between himself and his "runaway" people in Christ. Indeed, God had entrusted Paul with the message of reconciliation (2 Cor. 5:18–20). Paul therefore sends Onesimus back to Philemon with this letter.

In the letter, Paul first greets Philemon and the church that meets in his home (vv. 1–3). He then offers thanksgiving to God for Philemon's past acts of love shown to fellow Christians (vv. 4–7). His prayer for Philemon in verse 6 is offered in the hope that Philemon's faith will once again produce such love, as Paul prepares to present his appeal concerning Onesimus (vv. 8–22).

The Big Picture

In Philemon 1–7, the imprisoned apostle greets Philemon and offers thanksgiving to God for Philemon's love for the people of God and for his faith in the Lord Jesus.

Reflection and Discussion

Read through the passage for this study. Then review the questions below and record your reflections on this section of the letter. (For further background, see the *ESV Study Bible*, page 2355; available online at esv.org.)

1. Paul Greets Philemon (vv. 1–3)

While Timothy is mentioned as coauthor in verse 1, Paul's use of "I" in the body of the letter in verses 4–22 signals that he is the primary author. In light of verse 19, why do you think Timothy is mentioned as coauthor? What role did he possibly play in the composition of the letter?

While Paul does greet people other than Philemon (vv. 1–3), Paul's use of the singular "you" in the body of the letter in verses 4–21 signals that Paul primarily intends to address Philemon. If this is the case, it nevertheless remains true that Paul did intentionally greet the wider church family that met at Philemon's home (v. 2). Indeed, in the letter's conclusion in verses 22 and 25, Paul reverts to addressing the entire church (the pronouns are plural). Therefore, Paul has probably instructed Tychicus to read the letter aloud to the entire house church. How might drawing the larger Christian family into the letter—and the difficult situation it addresses—affect the situation? Is the issue between Philemon and Onesimus a personal one to be dealt with privately, apart from the wider Christian fellowship? Or is there something here that touches on the corporate nature of relationship in Messiah Jesus?

Paul's wish for the recipients of the letter is that they may receive "grace" and "peace" from God. Granted that this is a standard part of Paul's greetings in most of his other letters (e.g., Rom. 1:7; 1 Cor. 1:3; 2 Cor. 1:2; Gal. 1:3), do you think the wish is a throwaway? How might Paul hope God may use this brief prayer of blessing in the particular situation into which the letter is sent?

2. Paul Thanks God for Philemon's Love and Faith (vv. 4–7)

At verse 4, Paul transitions from greeting to thanksgiving. He conveys how he thanks God "always" when he prays for Philemon. As the apostle of the Gentile nations, Paul labored to fulfill this calling through regular intercessory prayer despite his imprisonment. What does the verse imply about Paul's view of the significance of intercessory prayer for gospel advancement?

Commentators agree that verse 6 is central to the letter. They also agree that it is notoriously difficult to translate. Paul appears to pray that the partnership or fellowship brought about by faith might once again become effective in Philemon's life. Individuals who place their faith in Christ are brought into a mutual union and familial relationship with other believers. Within this fellowship, the obligation to love one another reigns as the supreme virtue (compare Col. 3:14). On this reading of Paul's expressed prayer, how might Paul be laying the foundation for the appeal he is about to make concerning Onesimus in Philemon 8–22?

In verses 5 and 7, Paul expresses his joy over the love that Philemon had shown other members of the family of God in the past. By this love, Philemon had refreshed the hearts of those in need within the fellowship. With his mention of Philemon's past acts of love on behalf of needy members of the church, how does Paul continue to lay the foundation for his appeal concerning Onesimus— now a partaker of the fellowship in Messiah Jesus (see v. 20b)?

Read through the following three sections on *Gospel Glimpses*, *Whole-Bible Connections*, and *Theological Soundings*. Then take time to consider the *Personal Implications* these sections may have for you.

▶ Gospel Glimpses

GRACE. In the formal greetings of most of his letters, Paul wishes for and blesses the recipients with "grace." In so doing, the apostle has transformed the standard Greco-Roman epistolary salutation into a Christian formulation energized by and grounded in the cross of Christ. "Grace" is often defined as "divine unmerited favor," and the word certainly encompasses this idea. Often in Paul, however, the term can mean "divinely granted enabling power." Such "grace" empowers a disciple (or a community of disciples) to live a life fully pleasing to God. Paul prays "grace" for Philemon, as well as for the church that meets in his home, that they may have hearts that respond lovingly to the appeal he is about to make concerning Onesimus.

LOVE. According to Philemon 4–7, love is an overflow of faith in Christ that recognizes the community of fellowship created by that faith and gladly seeks to meet its needs. Love refreshes tired souls and produces joy and comfort in those who experience it. The ultimate demonstration of love was exhibited at the cross, where Christ died to set us free from sin and death and to reconcile us to God (John 3:16; Rom. 5:8).

▶ Whole-Bible Connections

"MY GOD." In Philemon 4, Paul writes, "I thank my God always." The phrase "my God" hints at the personal relationship that the apostle enjoyed and experienced with the God and Father of the Lord Jesus Christ. The apostle is probably echoing the language of the Old Testament, especially the Psalms. The phrase occurs there more than 50 times, revealing the psalmists' personal relationship with God.

THE LORD JESUS. The Old Testament hope included the day when God's Messiah would reign over all the nations of the earth. A majestic description of this future rule appears in Psalm 2. A royal psalm concerning the ideal Davidic king, it envisions a day when the Messiah will extend the kingdom of God over all the nations of the earth. Christ is this king (compare Psalm 2 with Acts 4:25–26; 13:33). Therefore, since Jesus is the world's true Lord, not Caesar, Philemon must not make his decision concerning Onesimus as a typical subject of Caesar. He must make it in light of the world's true Lord and his way of love and reconciliation.

▶ Theological Soundings

EFFECTIVE FAITH. While "works" are to be shunned in terms of how one enters and then sustains a saving relationship with Christ, it is also true that it is the nature of faith to "work." Paul wrote that he labored "to bring about the obedience of faith," meaning that he made every effort to make disciples whose faith expressed itself in obedience to the Lord (Rom. 1:5; 15:18; 16:26). Similarly, James teaches that a faith that does not "work" is dead (James 2:14–26). Faith always "works" itself out in a life of love (Gal. 5:6). Here in Philemon 6, Paul prays that Philemon's faith will once again become effective in love toward needy members of the fellowship. As we will see, Paul has in mind Philemon's own runaway slave, Onesimus.

KOINONIA. The *Oxford English Dictionary* defines *koinonia* as "Christian fellowship or communion, with God or, more commonly, with fellow Christians."

By virtue of his or her faith in Messiah Jesus, a disciple is brought into an indissoluble bond of fellowship and mutual relationship with other disciples. This fellowship involves both privileges and obligations. This kind of fellowship characterized the early church from its inception (Acts 2:42). It is energized by a shared faith in Jesus as the crucified and resurrected Lord of the world. It is characterized by active and united participation in the covenant community and its mission. It entails the sharing of the necessities of life when others within the fellowship have need. The bond that holds this *koinonia* together is love (Col. 3:14).

Personal Implications

Take time to reflect on the implications of Philemon 1–7 for your life. Consider what you have learned that might lead you to praise God, repent of sin, and trust in his gracious promises. Make notes below on the personal implications for your walk with the Lord of the (1) *Gospel Glimpses*, (2) *Whole-Bible Connections*, (3) *Theological Soundings*, and (4) this passage as a whole.

1. Gospel Glimpses

2. Whole-Bible Connections

3. Theological Soundings

4. Philemon 1–7

As You Finish This Unit . . .

Take a moment to ask for the Lord's blessing as you continue this study. Take a moment also to review this unit, to reflect on some key things that the Lord may be teaching you—and perhaps to highlight for review in the future.

WEEK 11: PAUL'S
APPEAL CONCERNING
ONESIMUS

Philemon 8–25

▲

Having greeted Philemon and the church that met at his home (vv. 1–3), Paul proceeded to thank God for Philemon (vv. 4–7). Paul was aware that God was powerfully at work in Philemon's life, for Philemon had overflowed with love toward needy members of the fellowship in the recent past. In light of these previous demonstrations of love, Paul begins his appeal concerning Onesimus in the hope that Philemon will once again act in love (vv. 8–12). Once a "useless" runaway slave, Onesimus had become "useful" as a beloved brother and treasured colleague in Christ. Paul desires, therefore, to have Onesimus with him to continue to assist him in his apostolic ministry (vv. 13–14).

There is, however, a problem. Onesimus had run away from Philemon and probably also wronged him somehow in the process (vv. 15, 18). Consequently, Onesimus and Philemon are estranged. Paul knows that to keep Onesimus for ministry without reconciliation between the two would undermine the very gospel of reconciliation that Paul preaches. Paul therefore sends Onesimus back to Philemon. However, the attempt at reconciliation is risky. Should Philemon refuse Paul's appeal, he could legally punish Onesimus severely (crucifixion was a possible option). Paul therefore introduces Onesimus as a "beloved brother," who now belongs to the family and fellowship of faith (vv. 15–16). If he is to remain faithful to the Lord Jesus, Philemon can no longer regard Onesimus primarily according to their Roman master-slave relationship. Philemon must regard Onesimus first as his "beloved brother" in the family of Messiah. In light of this new reality, Paul makes his appeal: "receive him as you would receive me" (v. 17).

▶ The Big Picture

In verses 8–22, Paul presents his appeal to Philemon concerning Onesimus, asking that Philemon welcome Onesimus into the community of faith as if he were the apostle himself (v. 17).

▶ Reflection and Discussion

Read through Philemon 8–25. Then review the questions below and record your reflections on this final section of the letter. (For further background, see the *ESV Study Bible*, pages 2355–2356; available online at esv.org.)

1. Paul Begins His Appeal concerning Onesimus (vv. 8–12)

Why do you think Paul refrains from using his apostolic right to command Philemon to do "what is required" (compare vv. 13–14)? As Paul prepares to make his formal request, how might his mention of his imprisonment and old age help to persuade Philemon to consent to the request (v. 9)?

What does it mean that Paul became the "father" of Onesimus (v. 10)? In light of this, how has the once "useless" Onesimus become "useful" and dear to Paul (vv. 11–12)?

----

2. Reason for the Appeal: Paul's Desire to Have Onesimus as a Personal Aide (vv. 13–14)

Before Paul makes his appeal, in verses 17–20, he first gives the reason that he desires Philemon to welcome Onesimus. If asked, no doubt Paul would reassert that reconciliation between Onesimus and Philemon was of eternally greater importance than whether Onesimus ever served as Paul's personal aide again. Nevertheless, what is it that Paul is asking of Philemon here? How does he ask? How does he hope Philemon will respond?

----

3. Introducing the New Onesimus: the "Beloved Brother" Forever (vv. 15–16)

In these two verses, Paul offers the reason he desires to have Philemon as his personal aide (note the "for" at the beginning of v. 15). What is the reason? How does what Paul says here pave the way for a possible reconciliation to take place between Philemon and Onesimus? How might it pave the way for a transformed relationship beyond the reconciliation?

----

4. The Appeal Proper (vv. 17–20)

In verses 17–20, Paul finally and directly makes his request. For what exactly does Paul ask? Our twenty-first-century sensibilities want Paul to ask Philemon for the emancipation of Onesimus, but is that what Paul requests? How has their relationship "in the Lord/in Christ" transformed the relationship forever?

5. Encouragement to Follow Through on the Appeal (vv. 21–22)

How might what Paul writes in verse 21 encourage Philemon to follow through on Paul's appeal? How might what Paul writes in verse 22 motivate Philemon to follow through on Paul's appeal?

6. The Letter's Conclusion: Greetings and Blessing (vv. 23–25)

Compare the people named within these verses with Colossians 4:10–14. Why do you think many scholars believe that Paul wrote the letters to the Colossians and to Philemon at the same time? (Compare also Col. 4:9 with Philemon 10.) Finally, why do you think Paul blesses the entire church that meets at Philemon's house with "the grace of the Lord Jesus Christ"? (The pronoun "your" is plural in Philem. 25.) How might Paul hope such "grace" will operate within their fellowship in view of the situation addressed by the letter?

Read through the following three sections on *Gospel Glimpses, Whole-Bible Connections,* and *Theological Soundings*. Then take time to consider the *Personal Implications* these sections may have for you.

Gospel Glimpses

PAUL'S IMITATION OF CHRIST. Paul's words in verses 17–19 reflect the essence of the gospel, as the apostle imitates his Lord in offering himself as a substitution for Onesimus before the wronged Philemon. Because of Christ's perfect substitutionary death on the cross, the Father welcomes repentant sinners as if they were Christ himself. In Philemon 17, Paul asks that Philemon welcome the guilty Onesimus as if he were Paul himself. In Christ, our sinful debt is charged to Christ's account (2 Cor. 5:21a). In Philemon 18, Paul asks Philemon to charge Onesimus's debt to his own account. In Christ, because of his perfect obedience, Christ is able to compensate God for our sinful debt (Rom. 3:23–25; Heb. 7:25–26). In Philemon 19, Paul pledges to compensate Philemon for Onesimus's debt. Paul lived to please and to imitate his Lord in a life of sacrificial love (1 Cor. 11:1). The life of every disciple is to imitate God's way in Christ (Mark 8:34; Eph. 5:1).

THE GOSPEL AND TRANSFORMATION. The letter to Philemon is an exhibit of how the gospel transforms lives and relationships. Formerly "useless" as a runaway slave who defrauded his master, Onesimus has been changed by the gospel of Christ. He is now "useful" as a beloved brother and personal aide to the imprisoned Paul. The gospel has also transformed the relationship between Onesimus and Philemon. Formerly related to one another as master and slave, the gospel has forged the two together as "brothers" in the family of God. The gospel insists that, while the previous relationship may continue (see Col. 3:22–4:1), it is to be transformed by the more important relationship established "in Christ" (compare Gal. 3:28). The *koinonia* in Messiah Jesus, with its obligations of love and reconciliation, must take precedence.

Whole-Bible Connections

THE EXODUS. God's deliverance of the Hebrew slaves from their Egyptian oppression stands in the Old Testament as the event that shaped Israel forever (see Ex. 12–15). Through the experience, Israel learned that God was the compassionate deliverer of the oppressed slave (Ex. 2:23–25; 3:7–12). Afterward, Israel annually celebrated the Passover, which recalled the exodus and reminded them that God had delivered them from their slavery in

Egypt. The prophets later picked up the exodus theme to announce that God would once again rescue his people in a "second exodus" in the messianic age. In Christ this redemption from slavery to sin was launched (1 Cor. 5:7b; Rom. 6:15–23; Col. 1:13–14). Any consideration theologically of slavery must reflect upon what these two "exodus" events reveal about God and his heart concerning the matter.

SLAVERY IN CHRISTIAN SCRIPTURE. It is difficult for Christians living in the twenty-first century to understand why neither Testament of Scripture explicitly commands the abolition of the institution of slavery. Both Testaments, rather, acknowledge the institution's reality and prevalence in the wider worlds of their day. Both, however, then seek either to provide instruction for how to humanize and regulate it, so as to prevent abuse (Old Testament), or to so transform the master-slave relationship "in Christ" that the institution would ultimately be subverted—at least within the church (New Testament). The abolition of slavery in the West came about in no small part because the gospel's influence had grown strong enough within the culture to help turn the tide. One should recall that in the first century, however, the house churches existed as a tiny minority in the vast Roman empire and held no power or voice to effect such seismic societal change.

▶ **Theological Soundings**

THE GOSPEL AND INSTITUTIONALIZED EVIL. While the church must always remain vigilant to not confuse the gospel for a manifesto of social justice, the gospel certainly leads Christians to speak with a prophetic voice to such issues as part of their overall vocation. Christians such as William Wilberforce led the charge for the abolition of the slave trade in the West in the eighteenth and nineteenth centuries. Yet now a new and insidious slave trade has silently grown to stunning proportions and requires the church to act once more. The global human trafficking industry now enslaves millions of people in its bondage. A lionhearted, new army comprised of those like Wilberforce must arise to confront this evil and labor to eradicate it from the earth.

THE PROVIDENCE OF GOD. God is continually involved in the lives of his people in such a way that they fulfill his purposes, without canceling out genuine human choice or moral responsibility. In verse 15, Paul writes to Philemon, "For this perhaps is why [Onesimus] was parted from you for a while, that you may have him back forever . . ." The verb "was parted" is passive and no subject is expressed. Yet most commentators have detected God at work behind the scenes. Onesimus made bad choices. He ran away from his master, and probably stole from him before he fled (perhaps to fund his passage to Rome). But God sovereignly worked in and through and despite these bad decisions to draw Onesimus to himself. In composing this sentence, Paul had the bigger picture in view of God providentially working out his epic rescue mission and plan for Onesimus and for the world.

Personal Implications

Take time to reflect on the implications of Philemon 8–25 for your life. Consider what you have learned that might lead you to praise God, repent of sin, and trust in his gracious promises. Make notes below on the personal implications for your walk with the Lord of the (1) *Gospel Glimpses*, (2) *Whole-Bible Connections*, (3) *Theological Soundings*, and (4) this passage as a whole.

1. Gospel Glimpses

2. Whole-Bible Connections

3. Theological Soundings

4. Philemon 8–25

▶ As You Finish This Unit . . .

Take a moment to ask for the Lord's blessing as you finish this study of Philemon. Take a moment also to review this unit, to reflect on some key things that the Lord may be teaching you—and perhaps to highlight for review in the future.

WEEK 12: SUMMARY AND CONCLUSION

▲

We will conclude our study of Colossians and Philemon by summarizing the big picture of God's message through these letters as a whole. Then we will consider several questions in order to reflect on various Gospel Glimpses, Whole-Bible Connections, and Theological Soundings throughout the two letters.

The Big Picture of Colossians and Philemon

Colossians

The imprisoned apostle Paul begins his letter by greeting the Colossian church. He thanks God for them because of the fruit that the gospel is producing in them since the day it arrived through the ministry of Epaphras (Col. 1:1–8). Paul then reports what he and Timothy pray for them, so that they might become pleasing to the Lord in every way (1:9–14). He then introduces a hymn that extols Christ's preeminence over both creation and the inaugurated new creation by virtue of his unique role in God's project of cosmic reconciliation. Paul introduces the hymn to explain to the Colossians that they demonstrate that they were swept up into this project when they display the telltale sign of reconciliation—persevering faith (1:15–23). Paul then explains the apostolic charge God gave him to bring the message of Christ to the nations and therefore why, despite his imprisonment, he is laboring for their church in warning them of the false teaching (1:24–2:5). He exhorts them to reject this false teaching, explaining that in Christ they have all they need for salvation and for their ongoing life with God (2:6–23). He exhorts them instead to become who they are in Christ, the last Adam, whose perfect image serves as the pattern for their own renewal as image-bearers of God (3:1–17). Paul then provides specific instructions for believers' relationships with members of their own household as well as with those outside and unfamiliar with the Christian faith (3:18–4:6). Finally, Paul concludes his letter. He passes on greetings from six coworkers and provides final instructions to ensure that the Colossian and Laodicean churches remain steadfast in the faith (4:7–18).

Philemon

The imprisoned apostle Paul begins his short letter by greeting Philemon and the church that meets in his home (vv. 1–3). He then thanks God for Philemon's love for the people of God, as well as for his faith in the Lord Jesus (vv. 4–7). Then, moving on to the body of the letter, Paul presents his appeal to Philemon concerning the runaway slave Onesimus, who has become a Christian. He asks that Philemon welcome Onesimus into the community of faith as if he were the apostle himself (vv. 8–25).

Gospel Glimpses

The gospel of grace is on full display in Colossians. God has effected a cosmic reconciliation at the cross through the blood of his Son, the Lord Jesus Christ (Col. 1:20). The message of this salvation is producing spiritual fruit all over the world as it spreads across the earth in expanding waves (1:6). When people embrace the gospel, God delivers them from the dominion of darkness and transfers them into the inheritance of light, the kingdom of the beloved Son (1:12–14). He redeems them, forgiving all their sins (1:14).

In Colossians the preeminence of the eternal Son over all things is revealed. Christ is the exalted Lord over both creation and the inaugurated new creation by virtue of his unique role in God's project of cosmic reconciliation (1:15–20). The preexistent Son entered history and became human. He reconciled his people to God by his death, that he might present them "holy and blameless and above reproach" before God on the last day (1:22). Christ is the very image of God, whose perfections serve as the pattern for their renewal as image-bearers. This transformative work is preparing them to inherit the new creational kingdom of God (1:12–14, 15; 3:9–10). Indeed, the gospel can be summarized as "Christ in you, the hope of glory" (1:27).

In Philemon, we see the essence of the gospel reflected in Paul's life as he imitates his Lord in offering himself as a righteous substitution for Onesimus before the wronged Philemon (vv. 17–19).

Have Colossians and Philemon clarified your understanding of the gospel? How so?

Were there any particular passages in the letters that led you to a fresh understanding of God's grace in Christ?

Whole-Bible Connections

The apostle Paul wrote Colossians and Philemon with the conviction that Jesus had brought the Old Testament epic story to its climactic fulfillment. This biblical epic of the kingdom mission of God runs from creation to new creation. God has launched the promised kingdom and new creation in Christ's death and resurrection.

In Colossians, Christ is the ultimate Son of David, the Messiah, and the world's true Lord. He is the fulfillment of all the messianic promises (Col. 1:13–14; 2:2; 3:1; "Christ" = Messiah). He is the Wisdom of God and holds preeminence over everything in creation as well as in the inaugurated new creation (1:15–20; 2:3; see again Prov. 8:22–31). The Son is the ultimate locus of the divine presence and fulfills all the Old Testament hopes for God dwelling among his people (Col. 1:19). In him the ultimate circumcision takes place, demarcating those who belong to the new covenant people of God and enabling them to live faithful lives (2:11, 13). Christ exists as the reality to which all the "shadows" of the Old Testament festivals and dietary regulations pointed (2:16–17). He is the perfect "image" and last Adam, whose own perfections serve as the pattern for his people's renewal as image-bearers (1:15; 3:9–10). This renewal prepares them for their vocation as citizens and rulers of the new creational kingdom to be consummated on the last day of history (see Revelation 21–22).

How has this study of Colossians and Philemon filled out your understanding of the biblical storyline of redemption?

Were there any themes emphasized in Colossians and Philemon that have helped you to deepen your grasp of the Bible's unity?

Have any passages or themes expanded your understanding of the redemption that Jesus provides, which he began at his first coming and will consummate at his return?

What connections between Colossians and Philemon and the Old Testament were new to you?

▶ Theological Soundings

Colossians and Philemon have much to contribute to Christian theology. Numerous themes are developed, clarified, and reinforced throughout the two letters, such as the doctrine of God, the sinfulness of humanity, the deity and humanity of Jesus Christ, and the eschatological kingdom.

Has your theology shifted in any significant way during the course of studying Colossians and Philemon? How so?

How has your understanding of the nature and character of God been deepened through this study?

What unique contributions do Colossians and Philemon make toward our understanding of who Jesus is and what he accomplished through his life, death, and resurrection?

What, specifically, do Colossians and Philemon teach us about the human condition and our need of redemption?

Personal Implications

God wrote the letters to the Colossians and to Philemon to transform us. As you reflect on these letters as a whole, what implications do you see for your life?

What have you learned in Colossians and Philemon that might lead you to praise God, turn away from sin, or trust more firmly in his promises?

As You Finish Studying Colossians and Philemon . . .

We rejoice with you as you conclude this study! May the truths learned here become part of your daily walk with God. Now we would encourage you to continue to study the Word of God on a regular basis. To continue your study of the Bible, we would invite you to consider other books in the *Knowing the Bible* series, and to visit www.knowingthebibleseries.org.

Lastly, take a moment to look back through this study. Review the notes that you have written, and the things that you have highlighted. Reflect again on the key themes that the Lord has been teaching you about himself. May these things become a treasure for you throughout your life—this we pray in the name of the Father, and the Son, and the Holy Spirit. Amen.